D0255553

Faithful Exiles: Finding Hope in a Hostile World
Copyright © 2023 by The Gospel Coalition

Published by The Gospel Coalition

The Gospel Coalition
P.O. Box 170346
Austin, Texas 78717

All rights reserved. No part of this publication may be reproduced, stored in a retrieval system, or transmitted in any form by any means, electronic, mechanical, photocopy, recording, or otherwise, without the prior permission of the publisher, except as provided for by USA copyright law.

Art Direction: Brannon McAllister
Cover Design: Spencer Fuller, Faceout Studio
Typesetting: Ryan Leichty

Cover Illustration: "Panel with Striding Lion," The Metropolitan Museum of Art, New York, Fletcher Fund, 1931.

Unless otherwise indicated, Scripture quotations are from the ESV® Bible (The Holy Bible, English Standard Version®), copyright © 2001 by Crossway, a publishing ministry of Good News Publishers. Used by permission. All rights reserved.

Scripture references marked NIV are taken from The Holy Bible, New International Version®, NIV®. Copyright © 1973, 1978, 1984, 2011 by Biblica, Inc.™ Used by permission. All rights reserved worldwide.

All emphases in Scripture quotations have been added by the author.

ISBN:
978-1-956593-09-9 (paperback)
978-1-956593-10-5 (ebook)
978-1-956593-11-2 (kindle)

Printed in the United States of America

FAITHFUL

EXILES

FINDING HOPE IN A HOSTILE WORLD

CONTENTS

CONTRIBUTORS

CLAUDE ATCHO is the pastor of Church of the Resurrection in Charlottesville, Virginia. He has previously served as a pastor in Boston, Massachusetts, and in Memphis, Tennessee. He is the author of *Reading Black Books: How African American Literature Can Make Our Faith More Whole and Just.*

ELLIOT CLARK (MDiv, The Southern Baptist Theological Seminary) served in Central Asia as a cross-cultural church planter along with his wife and children. He now travels around the world to equip church leaders and support residential missionaries. He is the author of *Evangelism as Exiles: Life on Mission as Strangers in Our Own Land* and *Mission Affirmed: Recovering the Missionary Motivation of Paul.*

ALEX DUKE is senior editor for 9Marks and the host of their podcast *Bible Talk*. He lives in Louisville, Kentucky, where he also serves Third Avenue Baptist Church as the director of youth ministry and ecclesiological training.

KERI FOLMAR lives in the Middle East where her husband, John, is the pastor of the Evangelical Christian Church of Dubai. She has written *The Good Portion: Scripture* and *How Can Women Thrive in the Local Church?* She is also the author of the *Delighting in the Word* Bible studies for women, including a new two-volume study on Romans. Keri cohosts the podcast *Priscilla Talk*.

MEGAN HILL is the managing editor for The Gospel Coalition. She is the author of several books, including *A Place to Belong: Learning to Love the Local Church*. She belongs to West Springfield Covenant Community Church (PCA) and lives in Massachusetts with her husband and four children.

JAY Y. KIM is lead pastor at WestGate Church. He's the author of *Analog Christian* and *Analog Church* and lives in the Silicon Valley of California. He and his wife, Jenny, have two young children.

BLAIR LINNE is known as one of the originators of the Christian Spoken Word genre. She is also an actress, Bible teacher, author of *Finding My Father*, and creator and cohost of the podcast *GLO* through The Gospel Coalition podcasting network. Proclaiming the gospel of Jesus Christ through writing and spoken word is her passion. She is married to her husband, Shai, and they have three children.

KEN MBUGUA is the lead pastor of Emmanuel Baptist Church in Nairobi, Kenya, and is the managing director at Ekklesia Afrika, a ministry that seeks to strengthen churches by providing access to theological resources. He and his wife, Arlette, have three children.

STEPHEN MCALPINE is the director for cultural engagement at City to City Australia. He is the author of *Being the Bad Guys: How to Live for Jesus in a World That Says You Shouldn't*. Stephen is married to Jill, and they live in Perth, Australia, with their two children. They attend Providence Church, a network of evangelical church plants in Perth.

BRETT MCCRACKEN is a senior editor and director of communications at The Gospel Coalition. He is the author of *The Wisdom Pyramid: Feeding Your Soul in a Post-Truth World*, *Uncomfortable: The Awkward and Essential Challenge of Christian Community*, *Gray Matters: Navigating the Space between Legalism and Liberty*, and *Hipster Christianity: When Church and Cool Collide*. Brett and his wife, Kira, live in Santa Ana, California, with their three children. They belong to Southlands Church, and Brett serves as an elder.

IVAN MESA (PhD candidate, The Southern Baptist Theological Seminary) is editorial director for The Gospel Coalition. He's editor of *Before You Lose Your Faith: Deconstructing Doubt in the Church*. He and his wife, Sarah, have four children, and they live in eastern Georgia.

SHANE MORRIS is a senior writer at the Colson Center and host of the *Upstream* podcast, as well as cohost of the *BreakPoint* podcast. He has coauthored hundreds of BreakPoint commentaries and columns and has written for *WORLD*, The Federalist, The Council on Biblical Manhood and Womanhood, and Summit Ministries. He and his wife, Gabriela, live with their four children in Lakeland, Florida.

JAIRO NAMNÚN is pastor of Iglesia Piedra Angular in Santo Domingo, Dominican Republic. He is married to Patricia and they have three children.

MIGUEL NÚÑEZ (DMin, The Southern Baptist Theological Seminary; ThM, Southern Baptist School for Biblical Studies; MD, INTEC School of Medicine) is pastor for preaching and vision at Iglesia Bautista Internacional and president of Ministerios Integridad & Sabiduría in Santo Domingo, Dominican Republic. He's a Council member of The Gospel Coalition and vice president of Coalición por el Evangelio. He has authored several books, including *Servants of His Glory: Cultivating Christlikeness in a World of Performance*.

GLEN SCRIVENER is an Australian author and speaker who lives in the U.K. He directs the evangelistic ministry Speak Life and has written 10 books, including *The Air We Breathe: How We All Came to Believe in Freedom, Kindness, Progress, and Equality* and *3-2-1: The Story of God, the World, and You*.

FOREWORD

THIS IS A CONFUSING time for Christians as they seek to best respond to the alarming trends they encounter in society.

Some give up the fight and choose to discard basic aspects of Christian belief and practice that run counter to societal trends. Others, overcome by disappointment, retreat from engagement in society and choose to simply, passively survive while trying to be true to biblical belief and morality.

Still others are infuriated by apparent defeats in the battle for righteousness as society yields more and more to the agenda of forces hostile to the Christian ethic. They resort to desperate measures of protest, using offensive methods in their quest to regain control. Sadly, they don't show signs of the "joy and peace in believing" (Rom. 15:13) that broadcast the gospel's beauty to our joyless and restless world. Their cause is right: countering injustice, immorality, and apostasy. But their methods don't commend their cause to a world desperately in need of the saving truth of Christ.

When Paul saw the impressive, beautiful temples in Athens, something else grabbed his attention. These magnificent buildings were devoted to idolatry. And he was enraged (Acts 17:16). But his approach to the people was restrained. He dialogued with them using the Athenian style of communication. Paul demonstrated the approach advocated by Peter, who taught that when we "make a defense to anyone who asks [us] for a reason for the hope that is in" us, we should do so with "gentleness and respect" (1 Pet. 3:15). We're provoked to anger by the challenges to Christian belief we face today. But we're restrained in our response.

We don't need to panic when we see segments of society being overrun by forces hostile to Christianity. Deeper than the world history we see, there's another history unfolding. God is working out his plan for his creation, and nothing can thwart it. The final victory, of which the resurrection is the firstfruits, will surely come in God's timing. We're living in the period between the firstfruits and the consummation. If we realized this, we wouldn't compromise our principles and accommodate ourselves to the present world. Neither would we use unbiblical methods to combat wrong. Our confidence in God enables us to stick within the parameters of Christian belief and practice.

The quiet confidence that comes from the vision of the sovereign God at work and the conviction we have a significant role in God's agenda would, on the one hand, save us from bitter hostility toward others. Such hostility is now being described as fundamentalism. It's incompatible with the peace of Christ that rules in our hearts and moderates our behavior (Col. 3:15). On the other hand, the knowledge God is at work will give us a passion to join in fulfilling God's plan for history.

The Bible is loaded with stories of people who, trusting in God, lived radiant lives of obedience under difficult circumstances and had a lasting positive influence. The book in your hands calls such people "faithful exiles" as it profiles several Old and New Testament characters whose lives have much to teach us today. It describes both men and women, people in different professions, and people facing hugely different challenges. Their faith in God helped them to be faithful. Presented here is a much-needed perspective on how we can be faithful to God in difficult situations. This book also challenges the apathy of some Christians who have given up on the possibility of making a significant difference in this world. It motivates them to join in the agenda of the kingdom of God during these confusing days.

Right now, my country, Sri Lanka, is going through one of the darkest periods in its history. The country is close to economic bankruptcy, with little prospect of recovery any time soon. A significant percentage of our population cannot afford adequate healthy meals. Impunity, incompetence, and corruption in high places have left people with no trust in the leadership. People have given up hope. Hundreds of thousands of people, including Christians, are trying to leave the country.

I've felt one of my most important callings these days is to promote the hope of the Christian faith in Sri Lanka. God hasn't given up on Sri Lanka. There's another history at work. If we align ourselves to the stream of

God's sovereign plan for the world—the other history—we move along a path that will ultimately lead to triumph. Amid the gloom that surrounds us, we can be excited about our call and give ourselves passionately to it.

In a passage that discusses how we should respond to the frustration we face on earth (Rom. 8:20–39), Paul says, "If we hope for what we do not see, we wait for it with patience" (v. 25). In the New Testament, patience is an active concept. Believing the sovereign God is working for good in all things (v. 28), we join with God in his work. So whether we're facing socioeconomic collapse as in Sri Lanka or cultural and religious upheaval as in the West, we don't retreat in discouragement or lash out in uncontrolled anger. Knowing God is working, we seek his will for us and resolve to do our part as his representatives on earth.

Ajith Fernando
Teaching Director, Youth for Christ
Colombo, Sri Lanka

INTRODUCTION

Elliot Clark and Ivan Mesa

"She who is at Babylon, who is likewise
chosen, sends you greetings." (1 Pet. 5:13)

WRITING TO CHURCHES ON the far side of the Roman Empire, the apostle Peter opened his first letter by addressing Christian diasporas (1 Pet. 1:1). These believers in Pontus, Galatia, Cappadocia, Asia, and Bithynia had been displaced and dispersed from their homeland. They were, in a real sense, *exiles.*

Yet their experience wasn't that of *literal* exile. It didn't involve their physical removal from a place. Instead, this exile manifested in social and familial ostracism. These Christians were marginalized and maligned for their faith. Following in the footsteps of Jesus, they were mocked and reviled (3:16). But also like Christ, they were chosen and precious (2:9; cf. 2:4, 6). They were, by God's grace, *elect* (1:1).

The twin themes of exile and election develop throughout Peter's epistle, culminating in its benediction. As Peter composed the final lines of his correspondence, alongside Silvanus and Mark, the apostle signed off: "She who is at Babylon, who is likewise chosen, sends you greetings" (5:13).

Of course, Peter wasn't writing from *literal* Babylon. By then, that infamous city—that ancient enemy of God's people—had long been gone. Yet by making this striking allusion, Peter connected with the experience of his readers. Just as they were *elect exiles*, he too was a chosen outcast. The church in Rome, of which he was a member, constituted God's chosen people in Babylonian captivity.

This creative turn of phrase does more than help far-off readers relate to the apostle. By depicting the church as God's chosen ones in Babylon, Peter reveals his understanding of the situation for Christians in all of life and in all the world. Wherever we find ourselves, we are exiles. Every citizen of heaven living on earth is far from home.

STORY OF THE BIBLE

In one sense, we could say such exile is common for humanity. Ever since the fall, sin has separated us from God and from one another. Part of what it means to live east of Eden is to experience the effects of sin's corruption, the corruption that touches every aspect of life for every person in the world.

However, God's chosen people have always experienced a particular and persistent exile. Abraham sojourned in Egypt. Moses ran to Midian. David fled to

Philistia. The nation wandered in the wilderness. Eventually, they were taken captive to Assyria and Babylon.

Some of their wanderings were owing to their sin, some to the evil of others or sin's curse upon the world (seen in human violence and natural disasters). Many of Israel's temporary homes were hostile locations that threatened their faith and their lives—which ultimately threatened the promises of God.

Today, God's new covenant people still experience a kind of exile. We may not be living in literal Egypt or Babylon, but each of us lives as a stranger in a strange land. Like John on Patmos, we're longing for the return of our King and the realization of our inheritance. This reality calls for patient endurance as we wait for the promise.

If this is the story of God's people from beginning to end, then the experience of exile will affect all of life. It will influence our prayer, our preaching, and our politics. But we must also recognize our exile isn't an accident. These fiery trials shouldn't surprise us. Instead, we recognize them as God's means for purifying the church and providing blessing for all the world.

Like Abraham's, our sojourn is part of God's plan—that the nations might seek and find their way to God (Acts 17:26–27). That Eden's exiles might one day make their way home.

PURPOSE OF THIS BOOK

Peter's first epistle, as an exhortation to fellow exiles, encourages believers to set their hope on God's future grace

(1:13). We can't think of a better goal for this book. Our desire is to give Christians *hope in a hostile world*.

There's no disputing that Christian beliefs, values, and ethics are in precipitous decline in the West. As many of us now inhabit a post-Christian society, we're learning for the first time what exile feels like. Yet this experience is nothing new for many believers and churches in the majority world. They continue to occupy spaces that overtly oppose their witness. As Peter wrote in the first century, such suffering is no surprise (4:12).

We want to learn from these brothers and sisters around the globe alongside those within the post-Christian West. We want to consider how God is at work in the world. We want to encourage you with a positive vision for how Christians can live in this hour of hostility. And we want to reflect on ways the church can respond to increasing antagonism, opposition, and threats.

By labeling our experience as *exile*, we're not implying the church is powerless. Nor are Christians exempt from social, cultural, or political engagement. Instead, we believe the gospel calls exiles to active involvement for the good of society while also directing us to gentleness and respect for all (3:15).

Is now the time for Christians to surrender the culture or retreat in isolation? Should we stand up and take back what's been lost? Rather than limiting our options to fight or flight, we believe the gospel gives rise to hope (1:3, 13, 21)—and that hope should color our actions and responses in every sphere of life.

To shade in that image of hope, we'll look at the lives of exiles throughout Scripture. Some of them were literal sojourners, foreigners, and refugees. Others simply lived as expats of heaven while strangers on earth. We'll consider their example as a model for how to live as those patiently striving for holiness while waiting for home (1:14–16). This is, in essence, the message of another letter in the New Testament: Hebrews.

Hebrews was written to encourage endurance in those tempted to succumb to social pressures. It was written so believers in a hostile environment might imitate "those who through faith and patience inherit the promises" (Heb. 6:12). To that end, the author of Hebrews famously recounted the stories of God's people in history who, in the words of C. S. Lewis, "did most for the present world" because they "thought most of the next."[1] Their story is our story.

This is the story of *faithful exiles*.

---

1.   C. S. Lewis, *Mere Christianity* (London: William Collins, 2016), 134.

CHAPTER 1

EXILE BEGINS

Jairo Namnún

"He drove out the man, and at the east of the garden of Eden he placed the cherubim and a flaming sword that turned every way to guard the way to the tree of life." (Gen. 3:24)

THE WAVES WERE STRONG but safe. The sargassum near the shore of our Airbnb meant we had to look for somewhere else to swim, so we found a beautiful beach just a mile or two from our rental. The white sand and turquoise water more than made up for the lack of accommodation. I was soaking it all in, watching my family enjoy an unforgettable day in the sun. However, I had to stay behind to look after the bags. This was a mostly unspoiled beach, away from the touristy part of Punta Cana. There was no security around the premises, and I know enough stories of friends wrapping up a great swim only to find their things stolen.

I live in the Dominican Republic, a small country in the middle of the Caribbean Sea. No matter where I go on our island, there's a beautiful beach a quick drive away—some of them counted among the best in the world, boasting homes the biggest celebrities frequent. And yet, while the beach is nearby and inexpensive, I hardly ever go.

The reason is exactly what you'd expect: life gets in the way. We have three young kids with school and activities to attend. We have jobs. We have dogs. What's more, I'm a pastor. We planted a church in 2022 that the Lord has blessed enormously, and the blessings of ministry usually result in more ministry. Preaching, yes, but also counseling and administration and meetings and visitations.

I need to be honest with you: I'm not a fan of the beach. I don't like sand. It's coarse and rough and irritating and it gets everywhere.[1] But my family loves the beach, my wife especially. And if I find good shade and get to sit down with a good book and a cool breeze, I can enjoy it too. Over the years, we've made some good memories at the beach.

I do regret not going more often. And I long for days gone by.

In this longing, I join our forebears, Adam and Eve. They, too, looked back at a time of beauty, safety, and companionship. Yet they also experienced, however briefly, what I haven't—a life with no death, a world without regret and without deceit. We don't live in that world, but

---

1. Yes, this is a *Star Wars* reference.

we do live under the same Ruler, so our forebears give us the first example of life under exile.

OUR FIRST HOME

The beginning of Genesis reads as if nothing could go wrong. In Genesis 1, God speaks, matter takes shape, and the universe falls into place. Yet suddenly, near the end of the chapter, there's a change of pace. God speaks reality *into* existence, then God speaks *with* humanity (v. 28), showcasing a relationship with humankind. After Genesis 1 details the forming, organizing, and establishing of the earth and the land and the sky and the sea, with all their beauty and splendor, the second chapter is dedicated fully to the creation of Adam and Eve.

In the garden, at the outset of civilization, man and woman are together—truly together: "The man and his wife were both naked and were not ashamed" (2:25). In them, the seed of all mankind was found. They were to "be fruitful and multiply and fill the earth" (1:28). All creation would be shepherded as they exercised "dominion over the fish of the sea and over the birds of the heavens and over every living thing that moves on the earth" (v. 28). What's more, they could have their fill and sustenance from creation (vv. 29–30).

God's plan was in motion. Through his Word, he's Creator of all. And through his words, he engages his image-bearers (v. 26). Consequently, Adam and Eve can speak words of faithfulness and companionship and commitment (2:23). Truly, everything God made was very good (1:31). A garden with no sin, no death, no defiance.

This is the world we were made to inhabit. Though our minds have no recollection of our creation and our brains have no memories of our first home, we were made from Eden's dust (2:7). We were created for beauty and splendor, for companionship and commitment, and for a close relationship with the Creator.

The beginning of Genesis reads like nothing could go wrong in God's world. But we live in a world where the most perfect beaches are filled with sargassum. You go out for a swim and your things can get stolen. The sun is hot, sand is coarse, and even if you find the best possible job and live in the most developed nation in the world, you're one phone call away from your whole life falling apart.

BEGINNING OF THE YEARN

As Genesis 3 brings a new character into the conversation, we're immediately brought down to a reality more like ours. The crafty Serpent lures the woman into conversation. Familiarity with the scene keeps us from grasping the gravity of what's happening. God's goodness and provision are being questioned. The very means of creation—his Word—is indicted. The Creator is judged by his creation.

Eve listens and is deceived. Adam joins her, and all humanity falls into temptation and sin:

So when the woman saw that the tree was good for food, and that it was a delight to the eyes, and that the tree was to be desired to make one wise, she took of its fruit and ate, and she also gave some to her husband who was with her, and he ate. Then the eyes of both were opened, and they knew that they were naked. And they sewed fig leaves together and made themselves loincloths. (vv. 6–7)

The effects of this moment would be felt by every human being. This is the dawn of our exile, put into motion in these verbs—seeing, delighting, desiring, taking, eating, and giving of a fruit of disobedience. As the Lord approached, Adam and Eve recoiled from his presence. They could no longer rejoice in him, and they were afraid (v. 10). They blamed everyone but themselves (pinning it on each other, the snake, and the Lord). But God is not mocked. The consequences of their actions brought a curse to all of creation, accompanied by a fresh and ever-present sensory experience: pain.

God said to Eve, "I will surely multiply your pain." And to Adam, he said, "Cursed is the ground because of you; in pain you shall eat of it all the days of your life. . . . For you are dust, and to dust you shall return" (vv. 16–19).

Can you feel how our exile began? It's possible—desirable, truly—to feel at home in the most undesirable circumstances. "Home is where the heart is" sells as home decor because home is about people—our loved ones—more than a place. But before sin brought the curse, before pain, and before death, Adam and Eve felt shame.

Sin led them to retreat from God instead of rejoicing in his presence. They were afraid of their Creator, and they blamed each other. There was no longer a sense of trust. In the absence of a loving relationship with each other and with God, how could they ever feel at home? The result is irrevocable:

> Therefore the LORD God sent him out from the garden of Eden to work the ground from which he was taken. He drove out the man, and at the east of the garden of Eden he placed the cherubim and a flaming sword that turned every way to guard the way to the tree of life. (vv. 23–24)

It was a mercy that God reached out to them as quickly as he did. And it was mercy that exiled them out of the garden. Left to themselves, we can only imagine what they would've made of Eden.

So mankind was cast out, and every boy and girl born after Adam and Eve has been born outside the garden. Let that thought sit for a second. We were created out of Eden's dust, in an idyllic garden where the Lord himself would stroll by our side, where animals would do our will, and where death wouldn't exist. But now we spend our days and weeks and months struggling in prayer. We're afraid of animals. Funerals are far too familiar. The curse has been so destructive—our exile so prolonged—that we don't even know how to find Eden, our first home.

This is life in exile, east of Eden, outside the garden. But not outside hope.

PEOPLE ON THE MOVE

A well-known Persian proverb says, "We come into this world crying while all around us are smiling. May we so live that we go out of this world smiling while everybody around us is weeping." I appreciate the sentiment: the desire to live a good life that influences those around us. But notice the uplifting message is underscored by pain: A new life brings happiness, but the baby is in tears of confusion and dismay. Meanwhile, a good death will always be surrounded by the tears of those who loved.

Since we don't live in paradise, even on our best days there's an undercurrent of unease. Suffering is never theoretical and never far. No matter how much we try to ignore it (and some of us are really good at it), there's been no human being ever born who hasn't experienced pain.

And yet the pervasiveness of suffering is a reason for hope for those in exile. When Elijah is persecuted because of his faithfulness and wishes for death, crying in his loneliness in the wilderness, the Lord responds that the prophet isn't alone: he's joined by 7,000 others (1 Kings 19:4, 18). To the church, we hear a clear command to resist the Devil, "knowing that the same kinds of suffering are being experienced by [our] brotherhood throughout the world" (1 Pet. 5:9). In Christ, our transient suffering is the fulfillment of his promise, a demonstration of his victory over the world (John 16:33).

If you're regularly singled out as the one who needs to do a "special assignment" for school or work while everybody else is enjoying his or her day, it's hard not to feel treated unfairly. But this exile experience—of being outside our home, uneasy, on the move, with suffering as a constant—isn't a special assignment. It's part of the job. And Christians find comfort in knowing our forebears felt it, the best prophets felt it, and our brothers and sisters all over the world are feeling it today too. As was promised to another of our fathers, those who are joining us in our pilgrimage are as many as the grains of sand on that beach where my family swam (Gen. 22:17).

So as we struggle with the sense of longing for another home, as we notice our souls yearning for better days, we must find rest in looking to our left and to our right and seeing with our spiritual eyes that we're joined by a multitude larger than the stars. What started with Adam and Eve and Elijah and Peter is true of Christians all over the world today: we've been exiled but not left to ourselves. We're not home, but we're not homeless.

RETURNING HOME

Every time I teach on Genesis, I'm asked some variation of the questions "Why did they sin? Why did they eat of that fruit?" Many better theologians have provided excellent responses, and one thing is clear: the human heart wants *more*.

Our desire for *more*—to create, to innovate, to build relationships and robots and rollercoasters—is in part because of God's image in us. But Adam and Eve's appetite for more demonstrated their distrust of God and discontentment with his good gifts. Just as the flaming sword turned every way, if our hearts aren't put in check—if our lives aren't submitted to his rule—God will continue to exile us with the flame of hell until sin is put in its right place.

Adam and Eve didn't leave Eden on their own; they were cast out. After their sin, they tried to hide, but there was no way out until they faced God. At the end of the day, all our struggles begin and end with the Creator. Because our first father and mother were created in his image, they *made themselves* a pseudo solution for their perceived problem immediately after they sinned. Likewise, when we find ourselves in inescapable situations, our hearts try to fashion a way out, to spin an upside.

But instead, we need to face the One who casts us out.

In their sin, Adam and Eve ran from God. They exiled themselves from his presence before he exiled them. Feeling his nearness, they must have noticed not just the gravity of their actions but the feebleness of their fashioned solutions.

"But the LORD God called to the man and said to him, 'Where are you?'" (Gen. 3:9). God doesn't play their games. He doesn't let them run away. He goes after his beloved, and he chases after us. Sin starts in us, but salvation belongs to the Lord (Jonah 2:9). Because there's no way home until we meet him, and because he's sovereign over Eden and earth, he is the One calling us to his presence.

Suffering is never far from us. Flung from Eden, we experience discomfort from life's first cry. No human being experiences life without death. That's the word of the

Lord to the woman and man. But it's not his only word. To the deceiving Serpent, he said, "I will put enmity between you and the woman, and between your offspring and her offspring; he shall bruise your head, and you shall bruise his heel" (Gen. 3:15).

The woman's offspring, born east of Eden, would experience pain and death. Jesus is that offspring, and suffering wasn't theoretical for him. He was "a man of sorrows and acquainted with grief" (Isa. 53:3). He too suffered exile, not only being hated by the world but also suffering "outside the gate in order to sanctify the people through his own blood" (Heb. 13:12). With his bruised heel, with his pierced side, he has opened a way back into the presence of God. So we can draw near with confidence, not shame, dressed in his righteousness, not clothes of our own making.

This is our present and constant hope. We're not alone in our exile; we join in the yearning of our forefathers since the beginning of creation. We have lost our home but not our family. We're not in the garden, so we lament. But while we suffer, we do so in the presence of him who was pierced to bring us back to God.

CHAPTER 2

CONTENDING AS EXILES

Glen Scrivener

*"By faith he went to live in the land of promise,
as in a foreign land, living in tents with Isaac and
Jacob, heirs with him of the same promise. For he
was looking forward to the city that has foundations,
whose designer and builder is God." (Heb. 11:9–10)*

WE HAVE REACHED A tipping point. The believer now lives in a "negative world"—and it's been that way for years.[1] Forces swirl at the cultural level; they dominate national and international affairs. Some of God's people are fighting back. Some are swept away. Others have gone AWOL.

---

1. Aaron Renn, "The Three Worlds of Evangelicalism," *First Things*, February 2022, https://www.firstthings.com/article/2022/02/the-three-worlds-of-evangelicalism.

At the same time, we face extraordinary personal and spiritual temptations. We're being seduced by sex, money, and power—and in unprecedented ways. It's a tumultuous age, and it feels like things will only get worse, at least for the next century or four. In the face of these mounting pressures, we contend for the faith, we cling to the Word of God, and we wonder whatever happened to God's promises for this land.

Welcome to the world of Genesis 14. In this chapter, we'll learn what it looks like to contend for the faith as a small minority surrounded by tyranny and temptation. Abraham will show us how to engage the wars of the culture without capitulating to tribalism or withdrawing to quietism. "The Abraham Option,"[2] as I'll call it, is neither passive nor pugilistic; it's priestly. And it's much needed in our day.

POWERFUL AND THE PERVERSE

Genesis means "beginnings." It offers the origin story, first of God's world then of God's people. The hinge point is in Genesis 11, where we turn from the global to the particular—from the nations to Israel. The Tower of Babel sums up all that's gone before: humanity in its pride. The people seek to make a name for themselves. But God resists the proud and lifts the humble.

---

2. For the sake of simplicity, I'll refer to "Abraham" throughout, though I recognize that in many of the accounts I highlight he's still referred to as "Abram."

He plucks Abraham from that same Babylonian region (and that same Babylonian mentality) to bring him west. It's *God* who will make Abraham's name great, and in a completely different way. Abraham will not be like the city builders who raise themselves up through works of the flesh. He and his offspring will instead mediate the downward blessing of the Spirit: *from* the Lord, *through* the people, *to* the nations (Gen. 12:1–3, 7).

By the time we reach Genesis 14, we're primed to see what happens when proud city dwellers collide. This is a chapter about war. But it's also about a tent dweller, Abraham, and the surprising ways he navigates the wars of his culture. As we explore Genesis 14, his situation may sound familiar to us. It's meant to. But first, let's meet the key players in this drama.

Genesis 14 is the Bible's first mention of "kings" and of "wars." Those two realities are very much linked. When there are kingdoms, there are clashes. First, we're introduced to the four kings: those of Shinar, Ellasar, Elam, and Goiim. As the Bible unfolds, these are the places from which most of Israel's trouble will come. The first three locations evoke the great Mesopotamian bogeymen of the Old Testament: Assyria, Babylon, and Persia. The fourth place, Goiim, simply means "nations."

You get the idea. These four Mesopotamian kings do in Genesis 14 what such kings always do in the Bible: conquer and enslave. But the powerful aren't the only threat to God's people. In Genesis 14, we meet another threat: the perverse.

The rulers of Canaan are much less foreboding, at least militarily. They occupy no heights. They are kings of the valley, little and low: "Valley of Siddim" (v. 3) means "Valley of the Plain"; "Valley of Shaveh" could be translated "Valley of the Levels" (v. 17). They're places of tar pits where their men fall (v. 10). Before destruction rains from above in Genesis 19, an abyss already lies in their midst.

In Genesis 13, the lowness of these cities is placed side by side with their sinfulness (vv. 10–13). They will become bywords for judgment and disgrace (Deut. 29:23; Isa. 1:9; Hos. 11:8), and the names of their towns mean things like "Destruction" (Sodom), "Submersion" (Gomorrah), "Red Earth" (Admah), and "Little" (Zoar).

These are the two blocs at war in Genesis 14: the powerful versus the perverse, the colonial versus the corrupt. But the winner—seemingly from nowhere—shocks everyone.

PRIESTLY AND THE POSSESSED

Abraham is the first person to be called a "Hebrew" in the Bible (Gen. 14:13). The word literally means "one from beyond." Hebrews are those weirdos from across the river. It's how non-Israelites would describe them (39:17), and it was a label they'd own for themselves (Josh. 24:2–15). They're strangers. Not the norm. They don't fit in. And if they try to (like Lot), it's always tragic.

Abraham is the original "stranger in town." As father of the Hebrew nation, he embodies all they're meant to be. And he couldn't be more different from the other nations. In a chapter about kings, it's striking that Abraham is never called one (neither is Isaac, Jacob, Moses, Joshua, or the judges). Abraham's household was almost certainly larger than, for instance, little Zoar. The Zoarites have a king, but Abraham is uninterested in the title. Abraham's militia outfights the forces of mighty Chedorlaomer, king of Elam, but still Abraham dwells in tents. Given he can call on 318 soldiers, we could assume his household contains 2,000 people, maybe more. Nevertheless, Abraham isn't, and never will be, a king. He's a family man: father to a household and "brother" to a wayward nephew.

That wayward nephew is worth considering. In Genesis 13, Lot and Abraham separate. Whereas Abraham lives by faith, Lot lives by sight—following his eyes to an Eden-like land. He chooses to live among great sinners, pitching his tent near Sodom (vv. 10–13). The next we hear of Lot, he's living *in* Sodom (14:12). This is the way of temptation. It always takes more from us than we intended to give. It draws us deeper than we were prepared to go.

Lot ends up not only possessed by the temptations of Sodom but possessed, literally, by the forces of Chedorlaomer and carried off. Lot may have been in the family of Abraham, but he remains a cautionary tale of what happens when Hebrews are *not* "ones from beyond." If members of the household of faith aren't distinctive, they become swallowed up by the perverse or the powerful, or both.

Thankfully for Lot's family, this calamity spurs Abraham into action. Now is the time for Abraham to contend against the powers of his day. But he took his time.

When the four kings conquer the five (v. 2), Abraham remains in his tents, camped by the oaks of Mamre. He's not battling the foe; he's building the family. When for 12 long years those Mesopotamian tyrants subjugate the Canaanites (including Lot), Abraham doesn't intervene. When the five Canaanite kings rebel in the 13th year, Abraham takes no part in it (v. 4). When the four kings fight back in the 14th year, Abraham is nowhere to be seen (vv. 5–10).

Only when Lot and his household are carried off does Abraham enter the fray. For the great majority of these 14 years of war and tyranny, Abraham is absent from the conflict. He's truly one from beyond—a stranger, foreigner, and exile. As Hebrews puts it, "By faith he went to live in the land of promise, as in a foreign land, living in tents with Isaac and Jacob, heirs with him of the same promise. For he was looking forward to the city that has foundations, whose designer and builder is God" (Heb. 11:9–10).

The Greek word for "city" here is *polis*, from which we get the word "politics." Abraham's politics were out of this world. He doesn't side with the four kings. This might have surprised his contemporaries since he too is from Mesopotamia and is a Shemite like Chedorlaomer. On the other hand, some may have thought he should side with the five kings—the Canaanites.

Certainly, Abraham's defeat of the four kings helps Sodom and the others. But no sooner does Abraham win victory than he distances himself deliberately and publicly from the five kings whose lands he's liberated (Gen. 14:21–24). His politics simply don't fit the expectations of the age. And this is because he favors neither the powerful nor the perverse. He is *priestly*, and he leads people to the only righteous king, Melchizedek: the king of peace (vv. 17–20).

The story ends not with smoking ruins or victory marches but with a meal of bread and wine and a prayer of blessing. Abraham brings all things not to war but to worship. Genesis 14 is a strange and wonderful story. But it's more than that. It's our story.

SCRIPTURE IS A FRACTAL

A fractal is a geometric shape that looks the same no matter the scale. When zoomed in or pulled back, the pattern remains. Perhaps search online for "fractal" or "Mandelbrot set" to see examples, because a fractal's *visual* structure is like the Bible's *literary* structure. You can zoom in on Scripture's details to find patterns at the micro level that repeat at every level. The little stories echo bigger ones, and the bigger ones fit into even greater plotlines that share the same features. Take Genesis 14 as an example.

Here we have Abraham, our Hebrew hero. He's just come out of Egypt with great possessions and into the land promised to him (Gen. 12). He's commanded to spy out his inheritance (Gen. 13). Then he makes conquest, defeating his enemies, running them off the land, and establishing true worship centered on the king of (Jeru)Salem (Gen. 14). The pattern is familiar, and it keeps repeating.

In the following chapter, Abraham is given this promise:

> Then the LORD said to Abram, "Know for certain that your offspring will be sojourners in a land that is not theirs and will be servants there, and they will be afflicted for four hundred years. But I will bring judgment on the nation that they serve, and afterward they shall come out with great possessions. (15:13–14)

As it is with Abraham, so it will be with his offspring. They'll be brought out of Egypt (Exodus), spy out their inheritance (Numbers–Deuteronomy), and conquer the land (Joshua), before establishing worship in Jerusalem (1 Samuel).

Zoom out further, and you see this is true of the definitive offspring of Abraham, Jesus (Gal. 3:16). Christ was brought from the hell of the cross to resurrection, and we await his coming again, when "the kingdom of the world [will] become the kingdom of our Lord and of his Christ" (Rev. 11:15). Don't stop there, though, because this pattern holds true for us as well. By faith, we're the offspring of Abraham (Gal. 3:29). We too have been delivered from our spiritual slavery, and we too dwell in this age as strangers in the land. We're heirs of the promise, waiting to inherit the earth.

Genesis 14 isn't ancient history. It reveals the shape of true life: the life of Abraham, of his offspring, of Christ, and of us. We see here a pattern for how to live as exiles in the present, contending for the household of faith amid the powerful and the perverse. Perhaps we could call it "The Abraham Option."

THE ABRAHAM OPTION

Abraham wasn't a king and he refused to prop up the power of kings. He wasn't a Babel-like builder of the city, nor a Lot-like sucker for the city. His eyes were fixed on "the city that has foundations, whose designer and builder is God" (Heb. 11:10). And while in Canaan, he radically devoted himself to the family of faith, knowing that, by the promise of God, his offspring was the hope of the world.

Having said this, we shouldn't think of Abraham as a mere quietist with no influence on his time and place. First of all, his devotion to the Lord attracted devotion from the nearby Amorites: Mamre, Eshcol, and Aner (Gen. 14:13, 24). Something about these strange Hebrews drew the locals who allied themselves with the household of faith.

Second, Abraham was clearly doing with his family what the Lord does with his people: he trains our hands for war (Ps. 18:34). For 14 years, Abraham kept out of the conflicts of his day. But in the meantime, he wasn't raising pushovers or aimless wanderers. Abraham's household of faith was dangerous. It could—and it would—make its indelible mark on the world. Indeed, it would conquer. But Abraham had the patience and prudence to know when to contend and how.

In New Testament times, of course, we're commanded to put away our swords of *steel* and instead take up the sword of the Spirit, Scripture (Heb. 4:12). We're to advance by persuasion and preaching, never by force or violence. Still, we're to advance. And military language isn't abandoned but rather repurposed: "For the weapons of our warfare are not of the flesh but have divine power to destroy strongholds. We destroy arguments and every lofty opinion raised against the knowledge of God, and take every thought captive to obey Christ" (2 Cor. 10:4–5).

As the offspring of Abraham, we still contend when the time is right. We patiently build the church, but at points we enter the fray of popular discourse when the household of faith is threatened. Our gospel confronts earthly powers, and at times we may be thought to "take a side" in this world's battles. But Abraham wasn't too much of a purist: sometimes he was entangled in his culture's wars. And he wasn't too much of a quietist: there came a point when he'd fight. As the children of Abraham, we too will fight. But we'll fight in a spiritual way. There are times when we engage the public square to "destroy arguments" and take thoughts "captive." Courage will be called for. In fact, more courage is required of a New Testament warrior, for we go to battle foreswearing all weapons and armor but clothed only in the Lord's (Eph. 6:10–20).

In the end, through sacrificial love, words of persuasion, and the cross of Christ, the victory is assured: "They have conquered [Satan] by the blood of the Lamb and by the word of their testimony, for they loved not their lives even unto death" (Rev. 12:11).

In Genesis 14, we see in miniature and in shadow how to contend for the household of faith. Abraham waited long years. But when his family was threatened with destruction, he acted. Lot's household was a target for the seduction of the perverse and the tyranny of the powerful. Abraham's household, on the other hand, was a quiver full of arrows, sharpened to make their mark (Ps. 127:4–5). In the public square (so to speak), the household of Abraham could "mix it with the best of them," even if they did so in unexpected ways.

The victory of Abraham's 318 soldiers should—if we think fractally—remind us of Judges 7, where the Lord gives Gideon victory—not with the 22,000 of worldly strength but with a paltry 300. In the West today, we might be daunted by the size of the missionary task and disheartened by our depleted numbers. But the Lord loves to give victory through weakness. And sometimes, as with Abraham or Gideon, he waits until the mismatch is overwhelming: like priestly trumpets versus the walls of Jericho; like Jael's tent peg versus Sisera; like David's slingshot versus Goliath; like Christ's blood versus sin, death, and hell; like the Spirit's Word versus Satan's strongholds; like a witnessing church versus the gates of hell.

From a human perspective, it's absurd. But with the 318 in mind, we regard things according to the Spirit and not the flesh.

WAY TO VICTORY

Genesis 14 climaxes not with battles but with bread, wine, and blessings (vv. 18–20). Where the warriors of the culture could think only in terms of triumph or tragedy, Abraham centered himself on a table. Here he found the one good king, Melchizedek: the King of Peace, the Priest of God Most High, and the Source of all blessing.[3] In *his* blessing, Abraham is able to disentangle himself from the battles he's fought.

For a time, Abraham picked a side in some earthly conflicts. He earned some powerful enemies, and he made common cause with some perverse allies. It was necessary to contend like this, and the Lord brought victory. But Abraham was last to warfare and first to worship. When the battle is done, he returns to the feast and to the family. There the Lord makes clear *he* is the One to build the household.

3.　In capitalizing these titles of Melchizedek, I'm pointing to his exalted significance. You don't have to agree with me that he's a Christophany (an appearance of the preincarnate Christ). But every Christian can agree he's a type of Christ. And when we read the Bible fractally, we can't help but be pointed to the ultimate King of Peace.

After the battle is done, we come to Genesis 15, where Abraham is a mere spectator and recipient. Here the promises of the Lord meet the fears of Abraham and his household. Do we fear the reprisals of the powerful? Christ is our shield. Do we fear missing out on the spoils of the perverse? Christ is our very great reward (v. 1). Do we fear the collapse of the church? Christ has promised offspring as numerous as the stars (vv. 2–7). Do we wonder how on earth he can bring this all about? Through blood-earnest, covenant love, the Lord will do it all. He will bring us through intense suffering to an immense inheritance. *Through* great affliction, the Lord will fulfill his purposes (vv. 9–20).

This is the pattern in every age. It's Egypt then promised land, exile then return, suffering then glory, cross then resurrection. The messianic people will triumph. But we triumph only and always in the way of the Messiah.

CHAPTER 3

HOPE AS EXILES

Keri Folmar

"For this is how the holy women who hoped in God used to adorn themselves, by submitting to their own husbands, as Sarah obeyed Abraham, calling him lord. And you are her children, if you do good and do not fear anything that is frightening." (1 Pet. 3:5–6)

I'M AN EXPAT. OUR family has lived in Dubai for almost 20 years. My husband is the pastor of an evangelical, English-speaking church, and it's been a joy to watch as people from all different backgrounds grow in the faith and come to know Christ in this majority-Muslim country. It took time, but a country that wasn't my own now feels like home.

Still, I'm often waiting. My children are grown and live in other countries, so I'm tied to my calendar, scheduling when I'll see them again. This type of waiting is exciting, but others are excruciating: Waiting to see what will happen to a family member diagnosed with dementia. Waiting for loneliness or depression to end. Waiting for difficult circumstances to change. Life is full of waiting. Often there's pain in the waiting, but for the Christian, there's always hope.

Sarah, the wife of Abraham the patriarch, lived a life of waiting. She was the ultimate expat. She waited for her travels to come to an end, for a place she could call home, and for a child to call her own. She didn't have an easy life.

When God called her husband, Abraham, to leave his country, family, and religion behind, Sarah obediently went with him. She, too, left everything. She left the way of life she knew. Together, they were sojourners, living in tents, in lands not their own.

Regular travel brought constant change and danger, including famine and potential enemies on every side. And Sarah no longer had little pagan gods to manipulate into providing her food and safety. Her husband worshiped the Lord, the God Most High, the One who made heaven and earth. This big God was now the only One to whom she could turn. She couldn't control him. He did things his way. Was he a God she could put her hope in?

WAITING FOR THE PROMISED SON

As we saw in the last chapter, God called Abraham out of his country into a land he would show him. God said he would bless Abraham, making him into a great nation. He promised that in Abraham's offspring all the nations of the earth would be blessed (Gen. 22:18). But there was one problem: Sarah was barren. They had no son to produce grandchildren. How would Abraham become a great nation with no heir? Sarah would have to wait on the Lord to fulfill his promise.

The Lord promised that Abraham's offspring would inherit the land. But Canaan's environment was as hostile as its people and as barren as Sarah's womb. When famine hit, Abraham took Sarah to Egypt. Fearing for his life, Abraham led Sarah to deceive Pharaoh, telling his men they were mere siblings. So Pharaoh took the beautiful Sarah into his house. Imagine Sarah's fear. What could she do? How would God fulfill his promise with her in the hands of another man? Abraham jeopardized Sarah and the promise, but the Lord rescued her by afflicting Pharaoh and his house with plagues (12:17). Abraham received riches and Sarah was given back to her husband. The Lord had done it. So back to Canaan they went with more sheep and donkeys and camels. And more waiting on the Lord to give them the promised son.

After 10 years in Canaan, Sarah took matters into her own hands. She decided on surrogacy. Turning her husband's leadership on its head ("Abram listened to the voice of Sarai," 16:2), she convinced him to take her servant Hagar to produce an heir. In language eerily like the fall of Adam and Eve, Moses tells us Sarah "*took* Hagar the Egyptian, her servant, and *gave* her to Abram her husband as a wife" (v. 3, emphasis added).

Hagar's pride swelled along with her belly, and "when she saw that she had conceived, she looked with contempt" on Sarah (v. 4). Sarah responded by blaming her husband and abusing Hagar, chasing her away. But God came to Hagar's rescue in the desert. Sarah had tried to do things her own way. She selfishly reasoned, "It may be that *I shall obtain* children by her" (v. 2). Now Hagar had a son, and still Sarah waited for the promised one.

Another decade of waiting went by. Sarah had gone through menopause. Her 90-year-old womb wasn't only barren—it was dead: "The way of women had ceased to be with Sarah" (18:11). But the Lord came again to Abraham and within earshot of Sarah told him their waiting was soon to be over. "The LORD said, 'I will surely return to you about this time next year, and Sarah your wife shall have a son'" (v. 10). Could it be true? Was the hoped-for son soon to come?

Surely not. Sarah laughed to herself at the thought of a worn-out woman, married to an old man, bearing a son. It's impossible! She had waited, but the Lord hadn't opened her womb. There was now no chance of conceiving. Instead of rejoicing at God's promise, Sarah's hope seems to have died along with her womb. But her lack of hope didn't thwart God's plans. The Lord confronted Sarah through Abraham, saying, "Why did Sarah laugh and say, 'Shall I indeed bear a child, now that I am old? Is anything too hard for the LORD?'" (vv. 13–14). Sarah denied her laughter even with the Lord's question ringing in her ears.

With only a year to wait, Abraham and Sarah once again took matters into their own hands. This time Abraham gave his "sister" to Abimelech. To save his skin, he endangered the wife for whom he should lay down his life, and Sarah went along with the scheme. But God came to the rescue again. He intervened to save his people and protect his promise, vindicating Sarah's honor in the process.

Finally, the time came when Sarah's waiting was over: "The LORD visited Sarah as he *had said*, and the LORD did to Sarah as he *had promised*. And Sarah conceived and bore Abraham a son in his old age at the time of which God *had spoken* to him" (21:1–2). Abraham was 100. Sarah was 90. God had made them wait. He'd put them in circumstances that made the birth of a son impossible. But here was Isaac, the promised son, life from Sarah's dead womb. Sarah's empty arms were finally full. God had said. God had promised. God had spoken. And now Sarah's laughter of doubt turned to laughter of joy for the baby nursing at her breast. Truly nothing is too hard for the Lord.

HOPE IN GOD

I wonder what you're waiting for. The degree or dream job? Meeting the right man? Double lines on a pregnancy test? The diagnosis or the cure? The pain to go away? Your loved one to come to know Jesus? The dreary cloud over life to vanish? Waiting is difficult. Like Sarah, we're tempted to do things our own way. Instead of going to

Scripture to remind ourselves of God's promises, we doubt his goodness. Rather than go to the Lord in prayer, we're pulled down into despair.

Sarah waited for decades. She faced difficulty and danger—and she dealt with her own sin. But God is faithful to fulfill his word to his people. He is the God "who gives life to the dead and calls into existence the things that do not exist" (Rom. 4:17). This is the God whom Abraham and Sarah left kindred and country to worship. He's the God who sustained them through famine and danger and dysfunction. The One who creates out of nothing is the One who promised them a son. And God keeps his promises. He is a God on whom we can wait.

Sarah is named a hero of the faith in Hebrews. Is this surprising to you? It doesn't mean she was a superhero. Her faith wobbled here and there. It even teetered on the brink. Like when she took Hagar and gave her to Abraham to produce the promised offspring. Or her reaction when the Lord said she would bear the promised son: "Sarah laughed to herself, saying, 'After I am worn out, and my lord is old, shall I have pleasure?'" (Gen. 18:12).

But Hebrews says, "By faith Sarah herself received power to conceive, even when she was past the age, since she considered him faithful who had promised" (11:11). God put Sarah in a place where it was clear that, apart from him, there was no way for her to conceive. She tried but couldn't make it happen. It was God who brought life to her womb. There were highs and lows in Sarah's life, like in each of ours, but Hebrews confirms the basic direction of her life was Godward. For all her stumbles, she was ultimately, through a journey of many years, characterized by faith.

So take heart. God is utterly reliable as we wait, even when in the waiting he calls us to do things that don't make sense. Imagine Sarah, 90 years old and pregnant. She belonged in the geriatric ward, not the maternity ward! But in the end, Sarah didn't look at her age, her physical condition, or her husband. She looked to God's promise and was given a son.

Peter uses Sarah as an example of a godly woman adorned not with external enhancements but with "the imperishable beauty of a gentle and quiet spirit, which in God's sight is very precious" (1 Pet. 3:4). She's the mother of all women who hope in God, all who "do good and do not fear anything that is frightening." She showed her hope in God by living a faithful life day to day with a disposition of submission toward her husband: "Sarah obeyed Abraham, calling him lord" (v. 6). Sarah waited, doing good and fighting fear. And the God in whom she hoped was true to his word. Not even her sin could thwart his promises. The promised son was born.

NOTHING IS IMPOSSIBLE WITH GOD

Thousands of years later, another promised son of Abraham was born. He's the One through whom the blessing of Abraham extends to all families of the earth. Just like Sarah's son, he was born in impossible circumstances, not from a barren womb but from the womb of a virgin.

(Nothing is impossible with God [Luke 1:37]!) Conceived by the Holy Spirit, he's not only the son of Abraham but the Son of the Most High. Jesus, Immanuel, God with us, who came to "save his people from their sins" (Matt. 1:21).

Out of his great love, God sent his only Son. Jesus lived a perfect life and died for the sins of anyone who would repent and believe. God, who gives life to the dead, raised Jesus, showing he'd conquered sin and death. We put our hope in this preeminent, promised Son.

Our hope is even more certain than Sarah's. She knew God was good. He had repeatedly rescued her. But we know God's ultimate rescue: "He has delivered us from the domain of darkness and transferred us to the kingdom of his beloved Son" (Col. 1:13). Because Jesus is alive, we who believe in the promised Son hope with certainty that we'll join him in the resurrection of the dead when he comes back to claim his kingdom.

Hope is for those who are waiting. As you wait, in what are you hoping? If your hope is in good test results, you can be seriously disappointed. If it's in a person or a family, it could bring you to despair. If it's in a career or your reputation, such hope can leave you exhausted. And even if these hopes come to fruition, will they finally satisfy?

Sarah didn't hope ultimately in her husband or in making Canaan her home; she "hoped in God" (1 Pet. 3:5). Sarah knew she was a stranger and exile on the earth (Heb. 11:13). She was "seeking a homeland" (v. 14), but that homeland was above. Sarah "desire[d] a better country, that is, a heavenly one. Therefore God is not ashamed to be called [her] God," the God of a weak, flawed exile, for whom he has prepared a heavenly city (v. 16). With the eyes of faith, Sarah had hope for a secure future.

Like Sarah, we mustn't set our hopes on the things of this world. God has "provided something better for us" (v. 40). The hope that comes in the Son will sustain you until all waiting is over. It's "a sure and steadfast anchor of the soul, a hope that enters into the inner place behind the curtain," where Christ is scated at the right hand of God, interceding for his people (6:19). We look forward to the city God has prepared, and one day Jesus will come and take us home.

This hope changes everything. When we're tempted by the pleasures of this world, we can instead do good because we know God "rewards those who seek him" (11:6), and his reward is greater than all the treasures of this earth. Even when we give in to sin, we can repent, knowing Christ has paid for all our sin and one day we'll "be made perfect" in him (v. 40).

When we're threatened as exiles, we don't have to fear what is frightening, because we know we'll "rise again to a better life" (v. 35). God has prepared an eternity for us, face to face with him. When we encounter difficulties of all kinds, we can persevere, knowing God is faithfully preparing us for the heavenly city "whose designer and builder is God" (v. 10).

The Christian life is a daily battle to put God at the center. We get so bogged down with details, we forget that every day brings us closer to eternity. Every battle with sin gets us nearer to perfection. These bodies that struggle and are wasting away will one day open their eyes to glory. Even now, Christ is our life.

HOPE THAT DOESN'T DISAPPOINT

So, like Sarah, set your hope on God. Set your hope on the future the promised Son has secured for you. Look to Jesus in the Scriptures and cast your burdens on the One who will comfort you. Read about women like Sarah and take heart. Consider God's "precious and very great promises" (2 Pet. 1:4). And dwell on Christ's death and resurrection, growing your longing for him. Meditating on the things of heaven will bolster your hope on earth.

I love that 1 Peter is written to "elect exiles" (1:1). As an expat, I can relate to living in a place that isn't my home. But whether I'm in the U.A.E. or the U.S.A., I'm an exile in this world. If you're a Christian, you're an exile too, traveling through a hostile world. In a letter written to a man named Diognetus from the second or third century, we read this description of early Christians: "Every foreign country is a homeland to them, and every homeland is foreign. . . . Their existence is on earth, but their citizenship is in heaven."[1]

Christians are those who look forward to a future home. Christ has secured its borders. Our only hope is in him, the Promised Son. Like Sarah's, our hope is in the

---

1.　Richard D. Phillips, *Hebrews*, Reformed Expository Commentary (Phillipsburg, NJ: P&R, 2006), 464.

God "who gives life to the dead and calls into existence the things that do not exist" (Rom. 4:17). That's a great hope indeed! "May [this] God of hope fill you with all joy and peace in believing, so that by the power of the Holy Spirit you may abound in hope" (15:13).

CHAPTER 4

HOLINESS AS EXILES

Shane Morris

"By faith Moses, when he was grown up, refused to be called the son of Pharaoh's daughter, choosing rather to be mistreated with the people of God than to enjoy the fleeting pleasures of sin." (Heb. 11:24–25)

WHEN MOST PEOPLE THINK of the story of Moses and the exodus, they're plagued by apocryphal details from one of several movie adaptations. Older generations may recall Cecil DeMille's *The Ten Commandments* (either the 1923 or 1956 versions) in which Moses has an Egyptian girlfriend.[1] Younger audiences may think of Ridley

---

1. Sruli Broocker, "11 Things the 'Ten Commandments' Movie Got Wrong," Jew in the City, April 13, 2017, https://jewinthecity. com/2017/04/11-things-the-10-commandments-movie-got-wrong/.

Scott's *Exodus: Gods and Kings* (2014), in which Yahweh appears as a little boy instead of as a burning bush.[2]

As a kid who grew up in the late 90s, I think of DreamWorks Animation's *The Prince of Egypt*. This cartoon epic supplies in artistic brilliance what it lacks in biblical accuracy (Moses is adopted by Pharaoh's wife instead of his daughter). But I'll always appreciate *The Prince of Egypt* for emphasizing one key theme of the biblical exodus story: how much Moses gave up by renouncing his status as Egyptian nobility to join his people in exile—and how he did it by choice.

We all know the basics of Moses's story, even if they're a little muddled by Hollywood's artistic license: Raised in Pharaoh's household, this foundling grows up beside the throne of the ancient world's main superpower. He hobnobs with the royal family, enjoys boundless wealth, and at least plausibly knows Egypt's crown prince (perhaps they really were like brothers!). Young Moses has the world at his command and a future blessed by the gods. This is all he could ever want.

Yet an inconvenient fact makes it impossible for Moses to maintain this charmed life: he's not Egyptian but Hebrew. In the Bible, he knows this from an early age, having been nursed by his real mother, Jochebed (Ex. 2:7–10; cf. 6:20). To add drama, *The Prince of Egypt* has him discover this as an adult. Cartoon Moses is horrified

---

2. Jonathan Merritt, "10 Inaccuracies Plaguing the 'Exodus' Movie," Religion News, December 19, 2014, https://religionnews. com/2014/12/19/10-inaccuracies-plaguing-exodus-movie/.

to learn his mother saved him from Pharaoh's genocidal rage by releasing him to the Nile and that his ancestors didn't worship Ra or Horus but the invisible God of Abraham, Isaac, and Jacob.

In both Scripture and fiction, this knowledge eventually prompts Moses to identify with his enslaved people and intervene physically in their oppression—an act that drives him, for the first time in his life, into exile. Still today, those who identify with God's people must make a similar decision to separate from the world and its desires for the sake of holiness. They must choose exile.

CHOOSING EXILE

The original story of Moses is told in the Old Testament. But speaking through the author of Hebrews, the Holy Spirit gives a fascinating summary. In the famous "Hall of Faith," we read this of Moses:

> When he was grown up, [he] refused to be called the son of Pharaoh's daughter, choosing rather to be mistreated with the people of God than to enjoy the fleeting pleasures of sin. He considered the reproach of Christ greater wealth than the treasures of Egypt, for he was looking to the reward. By faith he left Egypt, not being afraid of the anger of the king, for he endured as seeing him who is invisible. By faith he kept the Passover and sprinkled the blood, so that the Destroyer of the firstborn might not touch them. (Heb. 11:24–28)

We typically think of "exile" as a thing imposed, not chosen. And we associate it with punishment or chastisement for sin, usually for worshiping false gods. Yet for Moses, exile was self-imposed. Far from a punishment for idolatry, it was his road to becoming one of God's most faithful and treasured servants. This willingness to trade the luxuries of Egypt to become the spiritual leader of a nation of slaves resulted in painful personal exile. But it also led to a national *exodus*. We should dwell on the similarity between the two words.

In many ways, the entire story of the Bible is a series of exiles that end in exoduses. We might even call this the master narrative of Scripture. As I. M. Duguid writes in the *New Dictionary of Biblical Theology*, "The theological concept of exile is present virtually from the beginning of biblical revelation." In every story that follows humanity's expulsion from Eden, "the state of God's people is one of profound exile, of living in a world to which they do not belong and looking for a world that is yet to come."[3] And in exile, God's people always cry out for a deliverer, who arrives again and again to free them from bondage and lead them to the promised land.

Noah, Abraham, Jacob, and Joseph all undergo cycles of exile and exodus, often complete with salvation through water, plagues, a sacrifice establishing a covenant, and the spoiling of God's enemies. By the time

---

3. I. M. Duguid, "Exile," in *New Dictionary of Biblical Theology*, eds. T. Desmond Alexander and Brian S. Rosner (Downers Grove, IL: IVP, 2000), 475.

Yahweh delivers Israel in Exodus, they're "walking in the footsteps of the Patriarchs," treading a well-worn path and paving it for future generations.[4] This story of slaves delivered from bondage is the clearest exile-and-exodus cycle yet, containing both reminders of Genesis and rumors of redemptive history's far-off fulfillment. If we read carefully, we can hear themes in Moses's biography that echo in a greater Deliverer.

In Exodus, God's people are enslaved by a serpent figure who seeks to exterminate the seed of the woman, who nonetheless outwits him (Ex. 2:3). Her seed grows into a God-empowered deliverer who's given miraculous mastery over the spiritual powers of Egypt, culminating in a judgment of Egypt's sons (12:12), which the sons of Israel escape through the blood of a sacrificial lamb (vv. 13–28). The people plunder the kingdom of darkness (v. 36), undergo a baptism (14:22; 1 Cor. 10:2), and ultimately escape the forces of the serpent-king, which are put to open shame and defeated (Ex. 15:1–18; Col. 2:15). The deliverer then mediates a fresh covenant with God (Ex. 19:8), receives his law on a mountain (20:1–21), and prepares a dwelling in which God can at last descend to live among his people (40:34) and lead them into Canaan, a symbolic new Eden (Deut. 26:9).

In all this, Moses—who mediated the old covenant—bears a striking resemblance to the mediator of the new

---

4. Alastair Roberts, "Echoes of Exodus: Alastair Roberts (Dallas Regional Course)," Theopolis Institute, YouTube video, January 16, 2019, https://www.youtube.com/watch?v=WbQoTHJm89U&t=15s&ab_channel=-TheopolisInstitute.

covenant. We must pay special attention, because in imitating Moses, we're ultimately imitating Christ.

MOSES THE MERCIFUL

We're used to thinking of Moses as a lawgiver, not a Christ figure. In popular Christian imagination, the law is at odds with the gospel. Even *The Pilgrim's Progress* paints Moses as an adversary to Christian in his journey to the Celestial City. Moses beats Christian within an inch of his life for his "secret inclining to Adam the First." When Christian begs mercy, Bunyan's Moses replies, "I know not how to show mercy."[5]

To be sure, the law of Moses is powerless to save because of our sinful natures (Rom. 8:3). Bunyan is right about that. But in trying to make a point about our helplessness before the law without Christ, he portrays a Moses who bears little resemblance to the Moses of Scripture. The biblical Moses is an unmistakable type of Christ, mediating a gracious covenant in which God's people are spared from judgment by the blood of substitutes. Far from not knowing how to show mercy, Moses often pleads with God to have mercy on his people (Ex. 32:30–32; Num. 12:13).

Indeed, the exile-and-exodus pattern so clearly displayed in Moses's life is the very pattern the New Testament takes up when it explains the story of Jesus and our

---

5. John Bunyan, *The Pilgrim's Progress* (London: Simpkin, Marshall, and Co., 1856), 101.

redemption in him. Christ's story is filled with echoes of Exodus (Matt. 2:15; 3:13–17; 4:1–11; 5:1–2; 17:1–8; John 1:17; 1 Cor. 5:7; Heb. 3:5–6; 10:26–30). Christ became an exile to lead his people in a new exodus. In Moses's account, we see the gospel prefigured. "Christ," as Alastair Roberts puts it, "is the one in whom we see the true meaning of the Exodus."[6] This is why understanding Exodus in light of the Savior helps us better understand the role of the saved in a hostile world.

According to Hebrews, Moses *embraced* exile. He opted to seek Christ, forsaking the treasures of Egypt in favor of a heavenly reward. In seeking the Holy One and standing on holy ground, Moses accepted the loss of earthly riches and relationships. He not only relinquished his status as prince of Egypt but remained a kind of outsider from Israel for life. He was frequently at odds with the stiff-necked and grumbling people (Ex. 14:10–14; Num. 20:1–5; Deut. 1:26–36) and was even criticized and challenged by his own family (Num. 12:1–15).

In this, he personified the word often translated "holy" in the Greek Old Testament and the New Testament (*hágios*), which implies something "set apart," "different," or separate.[7] Moses was willing to stand out and stand alone so frequently—to choose enmity with the world and even with the people he loved—because

6.   Roberts, "Echoes of Exodus."
7.   Bible Hub, s.v. "Hagios," accessed February 8, 2023, https://biblehub.com/greek/40.htm.

he preferred friendship with God above all else (Ex. 33:11; James 4:4).

In the new covenant, we're all in Moses's sandals, enjoying close communion with a God who has come to dwell in our midst and call us "friends" (John 15:15), just as he called Moses a friend. This friendship with God need not always strain our earthly relationships. Yet when it does, Jesus is clear about where our loyalties must lie. We must be prepared to forsake "houses or brothers or sisters or father or mother or children or lands" when they conflict with our devotion to him (Matt. 19:29). We must do exactly what Moses did: embrace exile for the sake of holiness.

As the worldview and values of our society become less like Israel at its best and more like Egypt at its worst, this call to be set apart will become more frequent and urgent. Earthly riches, reputation, and relationships will often hang in the balance, tempting us to deny or keep quiet about our primary allegiance to Christ. Whether it's a promotion that requires hiding our faith, a grade that requires students to treat the Bible as false, or an invitation from a friend to celebrate an unbiblical union, all of us will at some point face the choice between earthly and heavenly rewards—between "the fleeting pleasures of sin" and "the reproach of Christ" (Heb. 11:25, 26).

COSTLY CALL

Not everyone is willing to pay such a high price. In the Gospels, Jesus encounters a rich young ruler not so different from a young Moses. When the man asks Jesus what he must do to inherit eternal life, Jesus recites Moses's commandments. "Teacher, all these I have kept from my youth," the ruler says. Jesus looks at him with love and pity and replies, "You lack one thing: go, sell all that you have and give to the poor, and you will have treasure in heaven; and come, follow me." Disheartened by Jesus's call to costly exile, the young man goes away full of sorrow (Mark 10:17–31).

Others have followed Moses's example of voluntary exile for the sake of Christ. William Wilberforce is another figure many will know from a Hollywood adaptation. (Thankfully, his movie is pretty accurate.) This 18th-century British politician and philanthropist wasn't adopted by royalty, but he was born to a well-to-do merchant family. His parents provided the best education money could buy, and in his youth, he became extremely popular. As one biography puts it, young Wilberforce was "witty, charming, erudite, eloquent and hospitable." Lacking Moses's clumsy tongue, he displayed "the charisma of a natural leader who drew friends and followers into his world."[8]

But Wilberforce's conscience, like Moses's, was eventually pricked by the plight of slaves. Following an evangelical reconversion, he famously declared God had set before him "two objects: the suppression of the slave

---

8. "William Wilberforce," The Wilberforce School, accessed February 8, 2023, https://www.wilberforceschool.org/updated-about-us/william-wilberforce.

trade and the reformation of manners [i.e., morality]." Under the spiritual influence of John Newton, a former slave-ship captain who penned the hymn "Amazing Grace," Wilberforce resolved the British trade in African bodies must end: "So enormous, so dreadful, so irremediable did the trade's wickedness appear that my own mind was completely made up for abolition. Let the consequences be what they would: I from this time determined that I would never rest until I had effected its abolition."[9]

And he never did rest. From 1789 to 1805, Wilberforce introduced 20 resolutions and bills against the slave trade, all of which were defeated through legal maneuvering by pro-slavery forces in Parliament. He endured withering criticism and death threats. He was attacked on the street, accused of being a spy in league with French revolutionaries, and even rumored to have a secret black wife whom he beat. Powerful opponents swore to fight the "damnable doctrine of William Wilberforce and his hypocritical allies."[10] Eighteenth-century pharaohs, like their ancient forebear, wouldn't part with their slaves willingly.

Yet Wilberforce persisted, weathering slander and chronic illness to accomplish his "great objects."[11] In 1807, the prayed-for day finally arrived. After years

9. "William Wilberforce," *Christianity Today*, accessed February 8, 2023, https://www.christianitytoday.com/history/people/activists/william-wilberforce.html.
10. "William Wilberforce," *Christianity Today*.
11. C. Ben Mitchell, "First-Person: William Wilberforce's Example," Baptist Press, January 23, 2023, https://www.baptistpress.com/resource-library/news/first-person-william-wilberforces-example/.

of half-measures and strategic advances, Wilberforce and other abolitionists in Parliament won overwhelming support for a bill to abolish the British slave trade. It was greeted with cheers and admiring tributes from colleagues. For the next quarter century, Wilberforce continued his fight to emancipate all remaining slaves, as well as keeping up a tireless effort to reform British society by promoting virtue, supporting charity, and improving conditions for chimney sweeps, single mothers, orphans, juvenile delinquents, and even animals. Convinced Christ had come to liberate spiritual as well as physical captives, he also supported missionary and Bible translation efforts.

On his deathbed in 1833, William Wilberforce finally received news that the House of Commons had voted to emancipate all slaves in the British Empire.

GREAT REWARD

Throughout Scripture, exile is usually imposed, not chosen. But rich and influential figures like Moses, Wilberforce, and the young ruler had a choice. All these men could lounge for a lifetime in their palaces and parliaments, rubbing shoulders with princes and prime ministers. They didn't have to surrender riches or reputation or endure the scorn that comes with pursuing holiness. Only two of them did so. Through the faith of Moses and Wilberforce, God led millions in exodus from bondage. We'll never know what he might have done through the young ruler who turned his back on Jesus.

Christians today face a similar choice. This foreign land is filled with strange gods and enticing treasures. Many of these treasures are good in an earthly sense, as are some things our neighbors wrongly worship (like sex and money). There's nothing wrong with Christians having and enjoying such things or with wielding the influence and authority Moses, Wilberforce, and the young ruler had. Yet a time will come when everyone who follows Christ will have to choose between treasures on earth and treasures in heaven. When the two conflict, the result will be a painful, costly separation—either from earth or from heaven.

On seeing the young ruler choose separation from God rather than separation from his money, Jesus observed there are few things more difficult than for the wealthy to enter the kingdom of heaven (Matt. 19:23). He spoke from experience. The true and better Deliverer was the richest of all voluntary exiles. He was in the form not of a prince of Egypt but of the God of the universe. This greater Moses "emptied himself," took on "the form of a servant," and became "obedient to the point of death, even death on a cross" (Phil. 2:6–8).

Why did he do this? Because he loved us, of course, just as Moses loved his people (John 3:16). But he also did it because, like Moses, he was after a heavenly reward—a great joy that brought him through the agony and shame of the cross and into the triumph of Easter morning (Heb. 12:2). In rising from the dead and ascending to the right hand of God, this true Deliverer led (and is leading) a spiritual exodus greater than any in history

(Luke 4:18) into a promised land filled with incorruptible treasure (Matt. 6:19–21).

If Christians with earthly wealth, influence, or reputation follow in the footsteps of Moses, we should expect to pay a high price. But like Israel's deliverer, who regarded disgrace for the sake of Christ as greater than the treasures of Egypt, we should also expect God to richly repay our choice. For all of time, he's brought about mighty, history-changing events through those who chase holiness till it hurts. And beyond time and history, he promises all who volunteer for exile a reward that would make Pharaoh jealous (Matt. 19:29; Rom. 8:18).

CHAPTER 5

WORSHIP AS EXILES

Ken Mbugua

"How shall we sing the LORD's song in
a foreign land?" (Ps. 137:4)

THE SUBJECT OF THIS chapter demands a biblical answer. How does someone worship God from a place of exile? Or, to hear it from the mouths of Israelites beside the waters of Babylon, "How shall we sing the LORD's song in a foreign land?" (Ps. 137:4).

Exile is a place where the clichés printed on mugs and bookmarks go to die. Since humanity's exit from the garden, God's people have experienced suffering in exile. So how are you coping? Where do you turn when living gets hard? And more pointedly, how do you sing praises to God from a place of loss or loneliness?

If hard times in your life correspond to lows in your spiritual life, I invite you to consider the full scope of the hope Scripture offers. It might well expose false hopes in your life and inspire more consistent worship despite your exile.

David was well acquainted with the realities of exile. He had to find refuge outside Israel as he fled from Saul (1 Sam. 20) and later had to leave Jerusalem when his own son Absalom declared himself king (2 Sam. 15:13–14). While those periods in David's life possess some answers to our question, the Psalms as a whole—and those of David specifically—play a crucial role in building the Bible's case for why we can worship as exiles.

In this chapter, we'll look at David's worship of God during his experience of exile and how that becomes a pattern for our worship through the Psalms, ultimately pointing to the new David who gives us hope and leads us home. As we'll see, the Psalms don't shy away from the bitter realities of exile. Instead, they step into the darkness of exile and teach us how to sing in the night.

DAVID IN EXILE

Taking a class from David on "Worship as Exiles" is like taking a master class from Steph Curry on making free throws or learning how to grill the perfect goat ribs from my friend Alex. David experienced exile in deeply personal and painful ways, but he was also "the sweet psalmist of Israel" (2 Sam. 23:1). David is the expert on our subject matter in this chapter. His class on worship as exiles comes from his difficult life experiences, from the pit of hard questions. Yet David finds solid ground for hope in

God's character, and he models for us how to make much of God in exile.

Before David became king, Saul repeatedly tried to kill him. Once, David had to escape from his home through a window (1 Sam. 19:12). For an extended time, the anointed one remained on the run. Like a wandering fugitive, he moved from city to city and cave to cave, avoiding Saul's fury and eventually ending up in enemy lands (1 Sam. 19–27). Later, after becoming king, David was again exiled from his home during the attempted coup of his son, Absalom (2 Sam. 15–18).

Exile for David meant tearful goodbyes to his dear friend Jonathan (1 Sam. 20:41). It meant fear for his life before kings (21:10–12) It meant concern for the safety and well-being of his loved ones (22:3). It meant feeling like he was alone in the world even though he was surrounded by people (Ps. 142:4). It meant being perplexed by what he'd done to deserve such trouble (1 Sam. 20:1). It meant living in danger of harm from those surrounding him (Ps. 57:4). And it meant experiencing mockery, insults, and shame at the hands of those who hated him (2 Sam. 16:5).

Exile is hard. David is our chief example of worship as exiles because he wasn't spared these bitter realities. Instead, they shaped his praise of God.

LAMENT

Instead of allowing the throes of exile to turn him inward in self-pity or to grumbling and complaining at others,

David turns to God with his complaints and protestations. David teaches us to come just as we are with our laments to God. This is the first expression of worship as an exile.

The hymnbook of the Bible (Psalms) has a myriad of laments woven into the songs and prayers offered to God. Our Lord, the author of the Psalms, wants us to know that in our troubles, the last thing he wants from us is lip service. Rather, God desires for us to draw near to him with our whole hearts and to pour out whatever is in our hearts. If in the hardship of trials, those are complaints, so be it. We're to take them to the Lord in prayer. So in the cave and on the run, David says, "With my voice I cry out to the LORD; with my voice I plead for mercy to the LORD. I pour out my complaint before him; I tell my trouble before him" (Ps. 142:1–2).

Perhaps your greatest expression of faith right now should be a lament that declares there's still a God in heaven to whom you can bring your complaints. That the God you pray to is a God who hears and cares, and therefore you can come to him with your concerns. Where faith cries to God, unbelief cannot abide.

So, afflicted saint, where do you take your complaints? What are your hardships on this side of Eden doing to you? Are they hardening your heart, or are they breaking you before God? Are you praying about what's in your heart, or are you filling your prayers with right-sounding yet empty words that flow merely from your lips? It's better to take the complaints you have about God *to* God than to worship God with dutiful lips and a distant heart.

Rather than merely determining to sing through the pain, learn the language of lament from David, and you'll offer to God acceptable worship in your exile.

IMPRECATION

David shows us how to worship God amid the injustices of exile. He was driven into exile because of the threat posed by a king he'd served faithfully and a son he'd loved dearly. In the case of Saul's threat on his life, David rightly asked Jonathan, "What have I done? What is my guilt? And what is my sin before your father, that he seeks my life?" (1 Sam. 20:1).

There are few things that have the power to deeply discourage us more than being on the wrong side of unjust treatment. How easy it is to grow bitter or be ruled by fear in those circumstances. How easy it is to lose all our joy and turn our meditations day and night to the wrongs done to us and to the dangers facing us from those who would do us harm. But David shows us a more excellent way: he entrusts himself to his sovereign Lord, to whom vengeance belongs.

When David had the opportunity to kill Saul in the cave, he chose not to take vengeance but rather to honor the Lord (24:1–7; cf. 26:7–11). Later, when David fled from Absalom, Shimei hurled curses at him (2 Sam. 16:5). Those around him offered to handle it, including Abishai: "Let me go over and take off his head" (v. 9). David's response, though, shows he's less focused on getting even and more desirous of entrusting himself to God (v. 10).

Although David wasn't willing to raise a finger against the Lord's anointed, he passionately cried out to God for justice in his prayers from the cave (Ps. 142:6). And as he fled from Absalom, he cried, "Arise, O LORD! Save me, O my God! For you strike all my enemies on the cheek; you break the teeth of the wicked" (3:7). These psalms give us insight into David's reasoning. The restraint he showed his enemies wasn't derived from a low sense of the evil of their injustices or from a pacifist impulse. David had a deep conviction that vengeance belongs to God, and thus to God he brought his plea for justice.

When we experience injustice in our exile, we, like David, are called to worship in light of this reality. The righteous anger we feel against evil governments that exploit the poor, abusive leaders who molest the defenseless, and greedy corporations that profit from unethical practices should be expressed not in lawless acts but in our worship as exiles. Like David, we cry to the Lord for justice, knowing the righteous Judge will destroy the wicked and establish his righteous reign forevermore.

REST

It's a grace that our lives aren't patternless plains of endless toil but that the Lord has allowed us the grace of rest even on this side of Eden. Every evening we rest after a day of toil, and every week God offers us rest after six days of work. These simple patterns are a shadow of the future rest awaiting us. So it is with our exile. The Lord in his mercy has apportioned graces along our pilgrimage.

If exile was all toil and no grace, none of us would make it safely home.

David had his friend Jonathan as he faced Saul, temple bread as he faced starvation (1 Sam. 21:6), the sword of Goliath as he faced his enemies (v. 9), and the loyal Hushai as he faced the treachery of Absalom and Ahithophel (2 Sam. 15–17). All these were gracious providences along his path to sustain him. For even in the wilderness, even in the presence of our enemies, God is able to set a table for us (Ps. 23:5). So it was for David as he fled from Jerusalem, away from the danger his son posed. We're told that "the king, and all the people who were with him, arrived weary at the Jordan. And there he refreshed himself" (2 Sam. 16:14).

The author of 2 Samuel makes a big deal of that river in the story of David's exile. The Jordan is referenced 13 times in the four chapters (16–19) that capture the story of David's exile and return. Crossing the river leaving Jerusalem reminds us of all the exiles in the Bible, like Adam and Eve's departure from Eden and Israel's exile from the promised land. Meanwhile, crossing the Jordan while heading home alludes to the promised rest offered to God's people. So it's noteworthy that the author here says David "there refreshed himself." The Hebrew word used is the same one found in the giving of the law, where the people were commanded to work for six days and rest on the seventh that they "may be refreshed" (Ex. 23:12; cf. 31:17).

How kind is our God that in David's weariness he provided rest. When all David should have been feeling was the weariness of exile, God gave him refreshment. God does the same for us. He hasn't stripped us of every grace. No, in Christ he's provided for us sufficient pit stops where we can gain the refreshment we need as we press on toward that heavenly shore. The gift of Lord's Day gatherings, of sitting under his preached Word, of an evening with friends, or even of modern medicine. These are all good gifts from God. And the Lord's good provision allowed David, even as he fled from Absalom, to testify, "I lay down and slept; I woke again, for the LORD sustained me" (Ps. 3:5). We can rest in exile knowing the Lord alone supplies all we need.

ISRAEL IN EXILE

One of the basic experiences of exile is the longing for home. Whether it's Pippin musing on "second breakfasts" or a refugee missing home as he struggles to adjust to a foreign land, the longing for home defines the hardship of exile.

I've often been entertained by watching Americans in Kenya enter a trance of sorts as they describe the different types of food they miss from back home. They appear to be momentarily lost in the ether as they describe the cheesy "this" or the crunchy "that" before they eventually come back down to earth or, more specifically, down to Kenya.

While some of our longings are little more than nostalgia, the Jews had painful memories. They were forcibly removed from their homes by the Babylonians. As they fondly remembered their homeland by the rivers of Babylon, their captors tormented them with demands to "sing [them] one of the songs of Zion!" (Ps. 137:3). The response of God's people in that moment captures the heart of the question we're faced with in this chapter: How do we sing when we're in a strange land (v. 4)?

We do well to grapple with this harsh paradox. For the Israelites, Jerusalem was the place of worship, but the temple had been destroyed. Zion was the city of God, but now they were exiles in a foreign land. How then were they to worship?

The psalm that follows begins to answer this question: "I give you thanks, O LORD, with my whole heart; before the gods I sing your praise" (138:1). God's people can and should worship the Lord in exile when surrounded by their enemies, when those around them are given to the worship of numerous other gods.

Then, in Psalm 139, we're given the answer, as it were, to the question of the exiles in Babylon—and of us today—by showing that the God of Israel isn't like the gods of the nations. Exiles can worship their God in any place because their God isn't tied to a house made with human hands like the gods of the nations. His presence fills the whole earth. Listen to David musing on the presence of God:

Where shall I go from your Spirit? Or where shall I flee from your presence? If I ascend to heaven, you are there! If I make my bed in Sheol, you are there! If I take the wings of the morning and dwell in the uttermost parts of the sea, even there your hand shall lead me, and your right hand shall hold me. If I say, "Surely the darkness shall cover me, and the light about me be night," even the darkness is not dark to you; the night is bright as the day, for darkness is as light with you. (vv. 7–12)

How can we sing songs of Zion by the rivers of Babylon? Because we cannot be so far away from home as to be far away from God himself. He is with us and has attached himself to our exile. That means our longing is mingled with some resting in God. Our darkness has some light. Our exile has a taste of home in it, for God is right there with us. So we sing despite the darkness, despite the pain, despite the deep longings for satisfaction. We sing because we're not forsaken. We've been united to God and nothing can separate us from him.

OUR GREATER DAVID

As we seek to learn how to worship as exiles, the goal isn't simply to look at the example of David. He doesn't perfectly display true worship, nor can he deliver us from our sin and suffering. Since exiles need more than a good example, we must look to the greater David, to the true son of David, who is the source of all our worship.

According to James Hamilton, this is who the Psalms have always been pointing to: "The Psalms, then, recount the history of Israel from David to the exile, and then

66

they look beyond the exile to the new David who will arise and lead the people back to the land."[1]

Even if earthly suffering has stripped us of any true companions or comforts, and even if we're far from home, we can have confidence our God is with us. Why? Because our greater David has joined us in our exile by leaving his Father's side and taking on our lowly human form. As a child, his life was threatened by kings (Ps. 2:1–2). As a man, he was betrayed by his close friend (41:9). And on the cross, he was forsaken by God as he suffered our condemnation for sin (22:1). But praise be to God, Christ didn't stay in the grave (16:10). After three days, the descendent of David rose from the dead and was declared to be the Son of God in power (Rom. 1:3; 2 Tim. 2:8).

For every saint in exile, this is the source of our song in the night. It's not that all our hard questions have been finally answered but that God has made a way for us to be rescued from our sin and reconciled to him. Exile is not our eternal lot. All who are in Christ know that soon—very soon—we shall, like him, be home again, where we shall see the King in all his glory.

So take heart in the comfort of God's character. Hope in the reality of his presence. And you too will be able to worship with David: "How precious to me are your thoughts, O God! How vast is the sum of them! If I

---

1.   James M. Hamilton Jr., *God's Glory in Salvation through Judgment: A Biblical Theology* (Wheaton, IL: Crossway, 2010), 279.

would count them, they are more than the sand. I awake, and *I am still with you*" (Ps. 139:17–18, emphasis added).

Our exile is not the end. Soon we shall cross the Jordan. Soon we shall enter into God's never-ending rest where we will worship him in never-ending praise.

CHAPTER 6

POLITICS AS EXILES

Stephen McAlpine

"And in the days of those kings the God of heaven will set up a kingdom that shall never be destroyed, nor shall the kingdom be left to another people. It shall break in pieces all these kingdoms and bring them to an end, and it shall stand forever." (Dan. 2:44)

THE FUNERAL OF QUEEN Elizabeth II in 2022 will be seen as the last great public acknowledgment in the West of a transcendence that limits temporal power. In our secular age, religion is reduced to a privatized experience. The public square declares "No heaven above us and no hell below." The Queen's funeral, replete with the language of temporal power being given by God, threw down a challenge to the rulers of this age: there is a God in heaven.

Such a challenge isn't new. And neither is the idea. We meet it most significantly in the book of Daniel, the exile template par excellence of the Old Testament. Daniel specifically states to King Nebuchadnezzar, "There is a God in heaven" (Dan. 2:28). This theme is repeated throughout the book, particularly in the narrative chapters 1–6, as are synonymous titles such as "Most High" and "King of heaven" (e.g., 2:18, 37; 3:26; 4:2, 37; 5:18). Daniel's message is a timely word for us today, as the West polarizes politically with a left and right divide, a divide mirrored in lamentable ways within the church.

LEFT-RIGHT DIVIDE

We're being pressed with two extremes in the political realm. First, there's the seemingly ascendant progressive political agenda that, as Mark Sayers puts it, "seeks to gain the fruit of God's kingdom—such as justice, peace, prosperity and redemption—but without the King."[1] The left craves human rights that are the fruit of the gospel throughout history but despises the roots.

Yet there's an equal and opposite push. Perhaps we could call it "Christendom without Christ." This is a move from the right that even some in the church espouse. It's a call for a return to the supposedly golden age of politics past, in which a Christianized culture set the political tone and agenda. We don't need everyone to be

---

1.   Mark Sayers, *Reappearing Church: The Hope for Renewal in the Rise of Our Post-Christian Culture* (Chicago: Moody, 2019), 24.

saved. That's not possible. But we should use temporal power to make the culture as "Christian" as we can—all within a democratic setting, of course. The trick is how to sell the product at a time when the percentage of church attendees is in decline and the percentage of "nones" and "dones" is on the rise.

The movements have more in common with each other than adherents would care to admit. Their actions either refute or negate the central truth that there's a God in heaven—an eternal Ruler above their temporal rule. The book of Daniel challenges both the growing hubris and overreach of secular progressives and the growing anger and frustration among conservatives, including religious conservatives. It does so by placing political power and political *impotence* within the reality of God's sovereignty.

The great irony in Daniel, concerned as it is with the physically and historically bound exile of God's people in Babylon, is that the book is shaped by God's transcendence. Six ripping yarns set within history, offset by a further six apocalyptic chapters. And even those first six give off apocalyptic fumes.

This is a prophetic challenge to those who hold the levers of temporal power: use them wisely. But it's also a pastoral comfort to those who realize those levers may never come our way again: lose them joyfully!

Daniel's lengthy life spanning several kings, and indeed kingdoms, reminds us the cultural exilic experience of God's people in the West may be a long-term reality. Cultural exile is the standard for God's people—our recent Western experience is merely the aberration that proved the rule. If this is the case, we need to gird our loins. The remainder of this chapter will explore three timely truths from the book of Daniel; truths that enable us to sail between the political Cyanean rocks threatening to crush the life out of our witness to our transcendent King.

1. GOD OF HEAVEN AS ULTIMATE REALITY

Long before we reach the famed Son of Man in Daniel 7, it's clear God rules over history, especially when his people seem to be on the wrong side of it. The book starts with the dreadful events of Jerusalem's destruction at the hands of Babylon's Nebuchadnezzar. Tragedy! Yet there's comfort amid it all: "The Lord gave Jehoiakim . . . into his hand" (1:2).

Heaven, it turns out, is less about God's postcode and more about his power. Even the dismantling of Jerusalem's worship system (v. 2), the capture of its political elite (vv. 3–4), and the reconstituting of it for Babylon's purposes and identity (vv. 5–7) come under his remit. All this before we ever read these words about earthly leaders in the book's second half: "As for the rest of the beasts, their dominion was taken away" (7:12).

Which is a reminder, of course, that their dominion was first *given*. That's where the rubber hits the road for Christians in the political sphere. All dominion is given. And if given externally, then taken away externally too. Not simply at the ballot box but by the God of heaven.

Christians shouldn't rage against the rise of political leaders with whom they disagree. They mustn't hate and scorn them. They need not. Even if there were no New Testament advice on how to pray for pagan leaders, there's the cast-iron truth of Daniel chapter 1: the Lord gives and the Lord takes away.

This means two things. First, Christians can call secular leaders to account with grace and humility. Even the tone and shape of our political disagreements must adorn the gospel. Second, Christians who find themselves in political power must maintain the tension of holding moral certainty with political reality. It cannot be the case that the winner takes it all. The fact that God is in heaven is a liberating reality for Christians as political exiles: it spares us the overreach we'll be prone to when we hold political power and spares us the despair we so often see in the evangelical subculture when power is lost.

Contrast our blessed position with those for whom politics has become the transcendent and for whom being on the "wrong side of history" cannot—must not—be countenanced. Self-proclaimed progressive author and essayist William Deresiewicz says such an idea is a "dangerous myth":

> The progressive myth of history also makes for arrogance and condescension. I said that the notion of history as a kind of force that blows through human affairs is like something out of physics—but really, it's like something out of Christianity. It is a secularized version of the Holy Spirit. "History is on our side" is

a secularized version of "God is on our side." "History will judge them" is an update of "God will judge them." To believe in the Holy Spirit is to believe that it acts through—that it fills—some people but not others. To believe in "history," in progress as a metaphysical principle, is to believe in the existence of a progressive class: the ones who push history forward, the ones who are filled with the future.[2]

Deresiewicz argues that this idea promotes transcendence without true transcendence or the kingdom without the King. In politics, ideas and attitudes yield results. Why does Deresiewicz call this myth "dangerous"? Because arrogance and condescension are the first steps on the path to political tyranny. All-seeing, all-conquering secular history ushered in the mass destructions of the 20th century in which a certain number (pick one) of reactionary eggs were to be broken to yield the perfect progressive omelet. Yet somehow, some still think they can open a fresh carton without breaking another dozen or so next time around.

But lest we think our only option is to quietly fold our wings and retreat to quietism while awaiting the return of Christ, the lesson of Daniel (particularly chapters 2, 4, and 6) reminds us, if we ever needed reminding, of the God who is *above* history yet works *in* and *through*

2.   William Deresiewicz, "There Is No Right Side of History," The Free Press, January 2, 2023, https://www.thefp.com/p/there-is-no-right-side-of-history.

history. The Christian faith is grounded on historical actions by a heavenly God—actions that can be observed and are consequential.

2. GOD OF HEAVEN AS HISTORICAL ACTOR

Politics in the modern West is willing to pay lip service to the gods in an ahistorical "thoughts and prayers" manner. The civic religion of the United States in particular is cemented in the deism of the Founding Fathers. Ancient Babylon, for all its idolatry and paganism, is little different. The king holds absolute power on earth. His word is divine in that it's final. He may have enchanters, magicians, and Chaldeans (Dan. 2:10), but the king brooks no heavenly rival. There's no Jewish prophet striding into the throne room with a "thus saith the Lord." When Nebuchadnezzar dreams, it's not from the domesticated gods of Babylon that help is derived.

Faced with impending death, Daniel urges his friends to pray to "the God of heaven" (v. 18), and it's "the God of heaven" (v. 19) whom he praises for the interpretation of the dream. It's "the God in heaven" whom Daniel announces to the king as the interpreter of dreams (v. 28). God interrupts Nebuchadnezzar's life to announce the God of heaven is God on the ground.

To live faithfully in political exile in the secular West means speaking truth to the power that pays lip service to a higher authority. It means trusting that earthly powers are limited in their reach when the time comes, and it will surely come, that they're directly challenged by the truth—whether or not they heed the warning. In Daniel 3, we see the true overreach of the king and his attempt to force history to his agenda. In sentencing Daniel's three friends to the flames for refusing to bow down to the towering symbol of cultural unity, the king asks, "Who is the god who will deliver you out of my hands?" In other words, "You're on the wrong side of history, the history I'm determining. All gods are mere constructs that bend to my will."

What was golden then is rainbow-hued now. The gender and sexuality agenda is being promoted as today's symbol of cultural unity. Overreaching legislators across the West are intent on getting all of us "on the right side" of political and moral history, on secularism's vision of what it means to be human and what it means to flourish. Woe to those who won't bow down to this particular idol. Our refusal beckons fiery denunciation, protracted legal and cultural hostility.

Yet the key reality—and it's a tension-filled reality— is the retort of the three friends who acknowledge that if God intends to, he could rescue them from the flames. The key caveat, however, is this: "But if not, be it known to you, O king, that we will not serve your gods" (3:18).

"But if not." To be faithful exiles politically may mean the price of faithfulness is we "lose." It may mean the culture "wins." It may mean, as with the three friends, the expression of the cultural king's face changes toward us (v. 19). It may mean we watch on impotently as un- godly decisions advance, negating time-honored truths around what it means to be gendered humans made in

God's image, for example. Across the West, Christian schools are facing defunding for holding to a biblical understanding of gender and sexuality. Health professionals are increasingly under pressure to simply "affirm" a client's chosen gender identity, while their professional bodies are demanding sign-off on values antithetical to a biblical ethic. Some professions will no longer be open to orthodox Christians. The courts increasingly take a dim view of religious arguments when considering start-of-life and end-of-life decisions.

One of the pressures we'll face, especially those who wish to be involved in the political process, will be to bow down to the supposedly unifying cultural idols of our day to advance ourselves and our causes. The rationale is that once we have the levers of power, we can pull them in a direction more to our liking.

This isn't merely about unfaithful accommodation to the left. The same is true toward the right. The "win at any costs" approach has pushed some within the evangelical camp to a place they shouldn't have gone. We're seeing the rise of a form of Christian nationalism that risks conflating the biblical nation of Israel with the modern secular state. Where this will end up isn't clear.

Political exiles allow the self-limiting reality of "suffer now, glory later" to set their agenda. In contrast to the "win at all costs" reality of modern politics, we see Daniel, in chapter 6, demonstrate where his hope lies. There he is, on the brink of greatness and ready to be declared second in charge of the kingdom, and yet he risks it all. Right there in the capital of the empire—the

Washington or Westminster of his day—he opens his windows toward the rubble heap of Jerusalem and prays (6:10). Why? Because he understands that's where his hope lies. Unless we have a conviction, like Daniel, that our hope lies in the salvation history of God, channeled through his people and coalesced in the person and work of Jesus—a man crushed in earthly terms by Jewish and Roman *realpolitik*—we'll balk at the loss of political power in the shiny earthly citadels. We'll forget it's through the church that God is doing his real and lasting work of restoring creation.

A friend of mine is the shadow minister for defence in Australia. His political star is currently bright. As one who acknowledges there's a God in heaven, he's realistic about the nature and promise of politics and understands evangelical Christians are viewed with an increasing level of suspicion in the public square. He's also aware that as a Christian he has the God-given opportunity to seek the flourishing of his "Babylon" and to love his neighbors and constituents, whatever their stance on faith.

As a former elite operative in Afghanistan, he has publicly spoken truth to power when war crimes by his own side were being investigated, and he received bipartisan praise for his integrity. As a senior member of a national parliamentary party, he has called for strong defense ties with nations who seek to uphold international justice.

But it's not all "big stage" stuff. He's convinced his local church—a small, seemingly inconsequential gathering of saints in his local working-class constituency—is where God is ultimately at work. So he ensures he's salt and light in his local community, meeting up with the many migrant groups who settle in these "hardscrabble" suburbs as they seek a financial and social footing. As their local representative, he seeks to rise above party politics.

His influence means he's involved in implementing change at the top of the tree and at the grassroots level. He's aware his clear Christian commitment may limit his political aspirations, particularly as secular hostility toward Christian ethics rises. Yet God is advancing his kingdom through his Spirit-filled, gathered people, and my friend knows he plays a part in that too.

Our faithfulness may win us the day politically. The cultural madness we're experiencing may be halted or at least slowed by our efforts, in the vein of William Wilberforce. But if not, we won't bow down to the cultural gods to achieve our agenda.

3. GOD OF HEAVEN AS SON OF MAN

Faithful political exile has a hope that neither sours into rage if its earthly agenda isn't realized nor demonstrates unpleasant hubris if it is. The backdrop of Daniel 1–6 becomes the foreground in Daniel 7–12. And we have this hope made more certain. The Son of Man's rule and reign over all history is assured for us this side of the cross and resurrection, whereas it was merely predicted for Daniel.

While Deresiewicz seeks to be irenic and generous in his assessment of political history, his article's heading—"There Is No Right Side of History"—is wrong. The resurrection, ascension, and session of the Son of

Man demonstrate that those of us who have bowed the knee to this ultimate Ruler are on the right side of history. Not because of our "rightness" but because of his.

This should transform both the ambitions and attitudes of our politics. There can be no "whatever it takes" for God's faithful exiles, because political history has been decided for us, not by us. We're not building a kingdom; we're receiving one (Heb. 12:28–29). We can take our place in politics with neither fear nor favor, trusting the outcome to the Son of Man before whom all political leaders will one day take the knee. We can lose graciously in politics because history isn't riding on the outcome of an election. There's a deep liberty to be had in serving faithfully, joyfully, and excellently in the political realm—not because we're the shapers of a history we all long for but because we're set to be receivers of such a history.

There is a God in heaven. One day his will shall be done on earth as it is there. And on that day, faithful political exiles will reign with him forever.

CHAPTER 7

MISSIONS AS EXILES

Elliot Clark

*"The Lord is not slow to fulfill his promise as
some count slowness, but is patient toward you,
not wishing that any should perish, but that
all should reach repentance." (2 Pet. 3:9)*

IN SOME SENSE, JONAH doesn't belong in this book.
He's certainly not *faithful*. Although Jonah eventually
follows through on his mission to Nineveh, he does so
begrudgingly. And while he experiences exile in various forms—even to the watery depths of the sea—it's
always self-inflicted.

Careful readers might wonder why Jonah's story
even belongs in the Bible. Among the literature of the 12
minor prophets, this work seems out of place. It's not a
record of judgment oracles or prophetic predictions. Instead, Jonah is a historical narrative. From beginning to

end, it reads more like the exploits of Elijah and Elisha from the book of Kings. However, unlike theirs, Jonah's example is largely negative.

Here is a prophet of God who doesn't heed the word of the Lord. While he claims to know and fear the Maker of heaven and earth, Jonah neither trembles before him nor recognizes his power. Instead, he tries to run from God's presence—as if that were possible. As a result, the narrative arc follows him *down* to Joppa, *down* to a ship headed for Tarshish, and eventually *down* to the heart of the sea and the belly of a great fish.

It's there where many people see redemption in Jonah's story. When he was at his lowest—in the womb of death itself—he cried out to the Lord. And the Lord delivered him, lifting his life from the pit. This experience of unmerited grace fills Jonah with gratitude. In the guts of the fish, his senses awaken. Jonah recognizes "salvation belongs to the LORD" (Jonah 2:9).

The problem is, Jonah also still seems to think salvation *belongs* to Israel. Because even after the fish spits him out onto dry land, even after God's word graciously comes to him a second time, even after Jonah goes to Nineveh and cries out against it, and even after the Ninevites repent of their wickedness, Jonah's anger is scalding. He's vexed that God would be merciful to the Ninevites—the exceedingly evil enemy of God's people.

In the book's final chapter, we learn this is the reason Jonah made himself an exile in the first place. He knew the Lord was "a gracious God and merciful, slow to anger and abounding in steadfast love, and relenting from disaster" (4:2). Jonah was more than happy to have a personal Savior who was gracious to him. He was content with a territorial deity who would mercifully bless his nation (cf. 2 Kings 14:23–25). What he couldn't stomach was the Lord of heaven and earth showing pity and compassion for wicked Assyria.

So he walks off in disgust, pitches a tent outside Nineveh, and waits for what he can only hope will be a reprise of God's volcanic wrath against Sodom and Gomorrah.

Here is another strange irony in this book. Not only does this prophet despise God's grace and disregard his word, but the positive characters of this short story are the pagan seamen and wicked Assyrians. They're the ones who demonstrate the pity of God, the divine compassion that seems so foreign to this prophet from Israel.

While Jonah comfortably sleeps in the ship, careless of the needs of others, it's the godless mariners who are concerned that none perish (Jonah 1:6, 14). And while Jonah comfortably reclines under the shade of his shelter, it's the despicable king of Nineveh calling for wholesale repentance that the Lord might "turn from his fierce anger, so that [they] may not perish" (3:9).

If Jonah is such a poor example, why is his story in the Bible—and why is it in this book? Because Scripture puts Jonah forward as a valuable lesson of God's gracious disposition toward all people, both his wayward prophets and the wicked nations. Jonah's story confronts the prejudice God's people often have toward their opponents whom they despise and fear. It helps us consider our call to be faithful and merciful as exiles on mission.

COMFORT OR COMPASSION

The story of Jonah reminds me of Nasreddin Hodja, a character from Central Asian children's literature. As the story goes, one day Nasreddin, a Muslim holy man, was lying under a walnut tree.[1] Looking up into its magnificent branches, he began to question the wisdom of the Creator. *Why should such a large tree have tiny walnuts? It could easily carry the large pumpkins that grow on spindly vines.*

Soon, Nasreddin fell asleep. But he was jolted awake when a walnut plopped onto his head. In that moment, he recognized not only the Creator's wisdom but also his kindness. While the Hodja was busy questioning the purposes of God, he'd been oblivious to mercy—the mercy that kept a falling gourd from crushing his head.

In Muslim folklore, Nasreddin Hodja is a silly and absurd character. But his puerile humor often reveals profound truths. Of course, absurd characters can be found throughout literature and throughout the world. Down through the ages, literary satire has been a sharp cultural tool to critique individuals and society at large.

---

1.   D. L. Ashliman, "Walnuts and Pumpkins," Nasreddin Hodja: Tales of the Turkish Trickster, Folktexts, revised May 16, 2009, https://sites.pitt.edu/~dash/hodja.html.

The power of absurdity is that it exposes reality. Such is the case in Jonah.

The name Jonah means "dove" in Hebrew, a name that seems to represent the silly and senseless nature of Israel (Hos. 7:11). Like the nation, Jonah is pitifully oblivious to the evil of his own heart and the unmerited mercy of God over him. While Jonah questions the wisdom of God in displaying kindness to Nineveh, he's blind to how that same grace has saved him.

This becomes clear in the final, climactic scene of Jonah's story. In his kindness, God appoints a plant—probably something like a large gourd or pumpkin—to sprout up and shade his pouting prophet. Amusingly, Jonah finds excessive happiness in the plant. But then God appoints a worm to kill the plant. As his beloved shade fades in the sun and withers in the wind, Jonah responds with rage. He's moved to both anger and pity. Pity for the plant—which is really self-pity. And anger toward the worm and the sun and the wind—which is really God-anger.

In that moment, we see the true character of Jonah. He's more concerned for his passing comfort than for the everlasting salvation of the Ninevites. His pity for himself, and for a perishing plant, overrides any compassion for the lost and dying among the Assyrians. Most concerning of all, he presumes on God's grace. Like many within Israel, he's somehow concluded God's favor *belongs* to him.

What the final chapter of Jonah reveals, then, is that his refusal to go to Nineveh stems from his disregard for

God's mercy, his desire for personal comfort, and his lack of care for the perishing. His story might be funny if it weren't true.

WARNING FOR EXILES

Henry Gerecke was an evangelical Lutheran minister living in Missouri in the early 1900s. At the outset of World War II, his two eldest sons entered the military. At 49 years old, Gerecke wanted to do his part, so he enlisted as an army chaplain, eventually working among Allied troops in the European theatre. However, his most notable service came after the war ended.[2]

When everyone else was eagerly returning home, including his sons, Gerecke received a letter asking him to stay behind. With his knowledge of the German language, he was a prime candidate to work among the Nazi prisoners awaiting trial in Nuremberg. Gerecke was asked to serve as chaplain to those who were, at that point in history, the most hated men on earth. The wicked of all wicked. It would be like Jonah going to Nineveh. And Gerecke agreed to do it.

Later, when the American press published his story, including Gerecke's willingness to graciously extend his hand to Nazi prisoners, he was excoriated. Back home, his service was seen as treacherous. But Gerecke continued. He quietly worked among the Germans for many

2.   See Tim Townsend, *Mission at Nuremberg: An American Army Chaplain and the Trial of the Nazis* (New York: William Morrow, 2014).

weeks, reminding them of the gospel of Christ and offering them the hope of life. As a result, in the last days before their executions, some of those despicable men seem to have come to genuine repentance.

If we're honest, the story of Jonah may seem completely irrelevant to us in the church. After all, what Christian would ever take God's grace for granted? Who among us would ever prioritize personal safety, security, and comfort over the salvation of the nations? What believer would ever entertain angry and vengeful thoughts toward the opponents of our faith? Or of our way of life? Or of our country?

We might assume Jonah's struggles would never be ours. But this is the power of satire. Its absurdity wakes us to reality.

The reality is that many of us in the post-Christian West are tempted to respond to encroaching exile with the spirit of Jonah. Living in a hostile world, it's easy to despise our enemies. Surrounded by opponents, the most natural response is to angrily fight for our rights. When others ridicule and threaten us, we're inclined to respond accordingly, selectively choosing who deserves our kindness—and in so doing, forgetting God's undeserved grace to us in the first place.

Instead of having compassion on the multitudes, it's easy to spend our time grumbling about modern-day tax collectors and sinners. But if the church is to be on mission, taking the good news of Christ to the world, we must beware the pharisaical spirit of Israel. This begins by acknowledging we're tempted to entertain the same prejudices as the prophet Jonah.

FROM JOPPA TO THE ENDS OF THE EARTH

For generations, Christians have recognized that the short story of Jonah speaks profoundly to our task of missions. It demonstrates God's call for us to go to the ends of the earth with the gospel. If God cares even for Nineveh, then the church must care for all the world. This necessarily includes those we fear, those who are enemies of our country, and even those who may hate us and hurt us.

Jonah's story also reminds us God is with us wherever we go (Matt. 18:18–20). In an almost comical fashion, this book reveals our God is truly Lord of all creation. There's no place we can go from his presence. Even in the remotest lands or deepest sea, he's there. This truth is the bedrock of all Christian confidence in missions.

Beyond that, Jonah holds out hope for Christian missionaries willing to go to the wicked and the worst. In this story—as in so many missionary stories—it's those seemingly least likely to repent who positively respond to God's word. Down through the ages, wherever the gospel travels, God always seems to have a people ready to hear (cf. Acts 18:10). The bigger question, it turns out, is whether his servants are ready to go.

Some 800 years after Jonah's call to Nineveh, God's word came to another reluctant preacher. It was Peter, and he was, of all places, in Joppa (Acts 10:5). In a vision,

Peter saw a sheet descend from heaven full of all kinds of animals and birds and reptiles (vv. 9–11). Three times the same image, and three times a voice telling him to kill and eat (v. 16). The very idea was disgusting. Peter couldn't stomach it (v. 14).

In that moment, the Spirit sent him to the home of a Roman centurion, a Gentile. It's an act that would've been unthinkable for any Jew in his day (v. 28). But Peter went, and we know the rest of the story. That very day, Cornelius and his whole household believed the gospel and received the Spirit, an event in church history that became the symbolic turning point for the advance of the gospel to all nations.

Today, we may not be in the exact situation of Jonah or Peter. Our Joppa can look very different. Yet whether we admit it or not, we're tempted to predetermine who qualifies for God's grace—especially when God calls us to take his gospel to our enemies: To wicked Assyrians. To Roman centurions. To Nazi generals. To Muslim terrorists, Hindu nationalists, or neo-Marxists. To the neighbor who mocks our faith or the transgender athlete who wins the race. To the mother who aborts her child or the activist who vandalizes our church. If our first instinct isn't compassion for them, we're already halfway to Tarshish.

The great danger for Christian exiles is that in their moment of self-protection and self-pity, they abandon God's love for the nations.

If we're more concerned about preserving laws and a way of life than about saving souls, we won't be effective in Christ's mission. As long as we're passionately pursuing our comfort and pleasure and security while the world is perishing, we'll never go to the hard places and reach the unreached. Instead, we'll see people primarily as potential threats or political foes, and we won't be concerned for their deepest need. Like Jonah, we'll be unfaithful to our task.

WORD OF HOPE

We don't know exactly when or how the book of Jonah was written, but apparently this unfaithful prophet returned from Nineveh having learned his lesson. Otherwise, why would he disclose such a personally humiliating account?

But Jonah's story is about far more than his silly and senseless actions. He's representative of a broader concern. His story is recorded to shape Israel's view of the world. Jonah was written to provide God's gracious perspective on Israel's enemies and to call his chosen nation to embody that same love and compassion for the world—even for Assyria, the nation that would ultimately lead them into exile. As such, his story not only belongs in Scripture but also has a place in this book.

We in the church shouldn't be so naive as to think we're all that different from Jonah or Israel. Those surrounded by enemies are often prone to spite and revenge. When we face existential suffering, whether political persecution or social stigma, it's easy to retaliate rather than forgive. We're tempted to seek our comfort rather than others' salvation. Threatened with exile, the natural response will be to abort God's mission for our own protection.

But Jonah's story is more than a word of warning. It also provides us with a word of hope. Hope in a God who calls sinners to himself. Hope in a God of second chances. Hope in a God of compassion toward the wicked and the worst. Hope in a God who uses flawed preachers to bring about faith among the nations. Hope in a God who is patient with us, not willing that any should perish but that all should come to repentance.

Hope for this hostile world.

CHAPTER 8

PRAYER AS EXILES

Megan Hill

*"On your walls, O Jerusalem, I have set watchmen;
all the day and all the night they shall never be silent.
You who put the* LORD *in remembrance, take no rest,
and give him no rest until he establishes Jerusalem
and makes it a praise in the earth." (Isa. 62:6–7)*

EVERY DAY, AN OLD man walks down my street. His head juts forward on a skinny neck, his back hunches with age, and his feet shuffle more than they step. In his hands, he clutches two small weights. With forearms at right angles to his body, he pushes dumbbells ahead of his torso. His progress is glacial. From my window, I can see him coming; minutes later, even after I've put in a load of laundry or started the dishwasher, he still won't be past my house. I've never met him, but he's become a familiar part of life on my street.

In a neighborhood of fast runners outfitted in sleek gear, this man is an oddity. His movement is slow, and his rumpled clothing isn't much to look at. But what impresses me is his faithfulness. No matter the weather, there he is, walking down the street, one foot in front of the other.

To temple attendees in first-century Jerusalem, Anna was probably a similarly familiar figure. "Here comes Anna," we can imagine the priests saying to one another as the old woman shuffled through the temple gate and across the courtyard, just as she did every day. The first worshipers of the day would stream past her on their way to pray; by contrast, Anna appeared to be standing still. She may have been slow, but she was always there. You could practically keep time by her. Anna was old, and Anna was faithful.

As we consider our own lives, Anna has much to teach us about what it means to be faithful over decades despite hardship and often amid loneliness. In particular, Anna shows us that God's people in exile ought to be people who pray.

EXILE AMONG EXILES

Anna's place in the Bible's story occupies only three verses. We meet her in Luke's Gospel as Mary and Joseph are bringing the newborn Jesus into the temple:

> And there was a prophetess, Anna, the daughter of Phanuel, of the tribe of Asher. She was advanced in

years, having lived with her husband seven years from when she was a virgin, and then as a widow until she was eighty-four. She did not depart from the temple, worshiping with fasting and prayer night and day. And coming up at that very hour she began to give thanks to God and to speak of him to all who were waiting for the redemption of Jerusalem. (2:36–38)

Anna's story may be brief, but we shouldn't underestimate her significance in redemptive history as a faithful exile—and her usefulness to us as an example.

The first thing Luke tells us about Anna is that she was a prophetess. God revealed his word to Anna, and she made it known to God's people. In this, Anna was unusual. She was a woman—and the Bible only describes a scant handful of women as prophetesses (cf. Ex. 15:20; Judg. 4:4). Perhaps even more surprisingly, she appears in Scripture at the end of the period between the Old and New Testaments. During these centuries—the so-called years of silence—the Lord hadn't spoken to his people by a prophet. For 400 long years, there had been no voice in Israel, and then, through the quavering tones of an old woman, God spoke.

The next thing we learn about Anna is that she was Phanuel's daughter and a member of the tribe of Asher. This, too, is significant. The tribe of Asher was one of the 12 tribes of Israel that became part of the northern kingdom when Israel divided under the reign of Jeroboam (1 Kings 12:16–21). As judgment for their rebellion, those tribes' land was destroyed by Assyria and their people taken captive. Anna's ancestors were alienated, conquered, oppressed, displaced, and scattered. Anna's people were among the "the lost tribes," the Israelite families who had been so dispersed as to become untraceable. In the eyes of many, those families had ceased to exist. And yet, 700 years later, Anna of the tribe of Asher shuffled across the temple court.

Luke then makes a third comment about Anna: she was very, very old. Whether Luke intends to say Anna was 84 or whether he means to make us do arithmetic and calculate her age to be around 105 (translations of v. 37 differ), the point is the same: Anna was "advanced in years." She would have experienced an extraordinary amount of hardship in her lifetime. Anna would have been alive in 63 BC when Rome conquered Jerusalem. She would have witnessed the city's siege, the temple's desecration, and the Jews' execution by the thousands. Like her ancestors, Anna experienced the terror and grief of being conquered by a hostile nation and seeing many of her generation killed.

Anna had also experienced personal loss. Early in her marriage, her husband died, leaving her in the precarious condition widows have shared throughout most of history. With no welfare system or social safety nets, Anna would have been dependent on the generosity of others—and the Gospels don't paint a rosy picture of the first-century Jews' inclination to care for the needy. In her old age, Anna was likely poor and vulnerable to mistreatment. She entered the temple gates every day in a position of weakness.

Most significant of all, Anna was looking for the Messiah in a time when few people were. We don't know how many Jews were "waiting for the redemption of Jerusalem" (v. 38), but Jesus's reception in first-century Judea suggests few were anticipating his arrival. At his birth, only lowly shepherds honored him. At his temple presentation, only two witnesses testified—declaring his identity as the Christ. Throughout Jesus's ministry, crowds may have followed him, but only a handful proclaimed him as Lord. Many in Palestine had given up faith, but Anna still believed Yahweh would fulfill his promise to send a redeemer.

In just a few verses, Luke demonstrates that Anna was an exile from among the exiles. A prophetess when there were no prophets, an Asherite when the tribal line was thought extinct, an old woman from a decimated generation, an Israelite in Roman territory, a woman without a family, a faithful believer in a faithless world. Year after year, the Lord had stripped away from Anna all the things that would have made her feel at home on the earth.

And every day, she came to his temple to worship him.

'SHE DID NOT DEPART'

Anna's life task was the work of persistent prayer. And when we, too, feel like exiles—when we live in neighborhoods and belong to families where it seems no one else shares our deepest convictions—we can learn from her.

Anna "did not depart from the temple, worshiping with fasting and prayer night and day" (v. 37). It may be Anna actually lived on the temple property, but it's likely Luke is simply saying she was a constant fixture in the temple—at worship whenever the doors were open. When God's people raised their voices in a psalm, Anna's voice joined them. When the teachers read the books of the law, Anna's ears were listening. When the priests offered sacrifices and prayers, Anna's heart remembered her own need for cleansing. Summer and winter, morning and evening, day after day, Anna worshiped.

And, most of all, Anna prayed.

Only in eternity will we know exactly what Anna prayed, but, as a faithful Jew, she would have asked the Lord to supply all her needs. As a prophetess, she would have called on the Lord on the basis of his Word. Surely she prayed for the Lord to preserve her life and the lives of others (Ps. 138:7), to supply food to the needy (37:25), and to give peace to her city (122:6). She likely prayed for the Lord to give his people work (128:2), financial provision (128:5), spouses (128:3), children (127:3), grandchildren (128:6), and long life (128:5–6). In this way, her prayers were probably not much different from many of our own.

But Scripture leads us to believe Anna's prayers were more than lists of temporal needs. Her commitment to fasting and her dedication to round-the-clock intercession over many decades points to prayers that rose above simple reactions to daily needs and desires. Anna's prayers weren't dictated by the concerns of the moment.

They were for the fulfillment of the greatest promise God had ever made: redemption.

Anna knew that what she and the rest of God's people needed was not merely a nice life, or even a life in their own land. They needed redemption from their sins, reconciliation with their God, and re-creation of their hearts. They needed the Messiah—promised to Adam and Eve in the garden and looked for by the faithful ever since. When she prayed, Anna asked Yahweh to send the Christ.

And Anna didn't give up praying. To pester the Lord like she did—day and night for decades upon decades—would be audacious, except God himself had commanded it: "On your walls, O Jerusalem, I have set watchmen; all the day and all the night they shall never be silent. You who put the LORD in remembrance, take no rest, and give him no rest until he establishes Jerusalem and makes it a praise in the earth" (Isa. 62:6–7).

Anna came boldly because God told her to be bold. She kept asking because God told her not to quit. Like another famous widow in the parable Jesus would later tell, Anna didn't stop begging God. And like that widow, Anna teaches us "always to pray and not lose heart" (Luke 18:1).

Exile is hard, and it's all too easy to allow the daily struggles of life in a fallen world to consume our prayers (or to keep us from the place of prayer altogether.) When we pray for decades for the salvation of loved ones, the growth of the church, and the revelation of Christ among people who aren't even looking for him, we rarely see quantifiable answers. Year after year, the world around us seeks hope everywhere but in Christ. Meanwhile, we exiles still need to get dressed, and eat, and pay the bills. Praying for the advance of Christ's cause in the world can seem futile, and, over time, our prayers dwindle to short lists of temporal needs or perfunctory requests without much expectation of God's answer. But Anna invites us to pray for more and to pray for it more often. She invites us to confidently ask God to do what he has already promised he would: redeem his people.

As we walk among people living in darkness, we can dedicate ourselves to praying God would shine the light of the Messiah in our hearts and theirs, giving new life and glorifying Christ. Anna's example also invites us to pray for the Lord's appearing, not as a baby this time but as the triumphant King. In the discouragement of exile, we need to fix our eyes on Jesus—looking expectantly for his work in the world now and for his final revelation one day soon. Like the saints of old, we keep praying, "Come, Lord Jesus!" (Rev. 22:20).

RIGHT PLACE, RIGHT TIME

Several years ago, our family took a trip to London. We spent our days touring museums, seeing the sights, and drinking tea. At one point, we were walking down a street when the police abruptly closed off the roadway. Soon, a motorcade made its way past. We asked a fellow bystander what was happening, and he told us Prince William was in one of the cars.

As I peered through the vehicles' tinted windows, I realized I had a problem. Each car's backseat held a well-dressed man, and I didn't know what Prince William looked like. If I'd been prepared, I would have Googled pictures before I ever set foot on that street. As it was, I was ignorant. I *saw* the prince that day, but I didn't recognize him because I wasn't ready to look for him.

Anna didn't have this problem. She'd been preparing for a lifetime to see the Messiah, and when he appeared, she was ready. "Coming up at that very hour" (Luke 2:38), Anna saw a helpless newborn and recognized him as the Christ because she'd been looking for him with the eyes of faith for decades.

Over her lifetime, Anna would have treasured the prophecy of Malachi: "Behold, I send my messenger, and he will prepare the way before me. And the Lord whom you seek will suddenly come to his temple; and the messenger of the covenant in whom you delight, behold, he is coming, says the LORD of hosts" (Mal. 3:1).

Who knows, maybe Anna had witnessed the moment, just months prior to the events of Luke 2, when Zechariah staggered, wordless, out of the temple's holy place with the seed of the Messiah's herald in his body. Who knows but that this answer to Anna's prayers had given her fresh energy to keep praying for the second half of that promise—asking the Lord himself to come into the very temple where she sought him. Who knows but that she wasn't surprised at all when he did.

We, too, can have confidence we'll experience Christ's presence when we seek him in prayer. God's words through Jeremiah would have been familiar to Anna, and they should be familiar to us: "You will seek me and find me, when you seek me with all your heart" (29:13). In our seasons of exile, when we feel displaced and alone in a world that's certainly not seeking the Messiah, we have his sure and certain promise he'll be found by all who seek his face.

As we pray in secret (Matt. 6:6) and with others (18:20), the Lord draws near to us. In answer to our prayers, the Redeemer of the elect pours out his Spirit in our midst: giving power to his Word (1 Thess. 1:5), convicting us of sin (John 16:8), granting new life (3:6), stirring us to praise (Eph. 5:18–19), enabling us to obey (Rom. 8:4), and helping us to keep praying (v. 26).

The Lord's works are often unnoticed by the world—like the presence of a newborn baby in a crowd—but, with the eyes of faith, we'll see and rejoice. When we look for him in prayer, Christ will be found. Anna shows us the life of faithfulness is marked by being in the right place at the right time—not in human strength but on our knees, not by accident but by intent.

The verses of Anna's story begin with exile, but they end in community—Anna, the prophetess of the tribe of Asher, the remnant of the remnant,[1] announced the Messiah's coming to all who were likewise waiting. The faithful gathered around the old woman and heard the

---

1. "A remnant of a remnant" is a lovely description of Anna that I borrowed (and tweaked) from Martyn McGeown, *Born for Our Salvation: The Nativity and Childhood of Jesus Christ* (Jenison, MI: Reformed Free Publishing Association, 2019), 167.

news from her lips: "The Lord has come into his temple!" Surely there were shouts of joy, tears, kisses, and hugs. Surely there were prayers of thanksgiving.

Our story, too, will end in a glorious gathering. One day soon, we'll be part of that "great multitude that no one could number, from every nation, from all tribes and peoples and languages" (Rev. 7:9). The redeemed exiles will gather before the throne of Christ, and we'll behold him. Faith will become sight, and our voices will join the shout of praise: "Salvation belongs to our God who sits on the throne, and to the Lamb!" (v. 10). One day soon, all our prayers will receive their answer, and we'll be forever with the Lord.

CHAPTER 9

PREACHING AS EXILES

Miguel Núñez

"The voice of one crying in the wilderness:
'Prepare the way of the Lord, make his
paths straight.'" (Mark 1:3)

WHEN PEOPLE CHOOSE A career, they want to make a living. Most also want to make a difference. Future doctors undergo the rigors of medical school not just for the future paycheck but because they desire to serve the sick. And as an aspiring physician, you assume you'll never lack for patients.

The same is true for aspiring preachers. You go to seminary, learning how to understand and communicate God's Word, all the while presuming an audience. The unspoken assumption in most homiletics classes is there will always be people in the pews.

But what happens when your message becomes unpopular? Or when those who once appreciated your preaching no longer do? Or when the Lord decides to bring a period of spiritual dryness upon the people in his desire to bring them back to him? Preachers can't always expect loyal listeners, sermon subscribers, or sincere seekers. When we look to Scripture, we see a long list of prophetic witnesses who were rejected by the surrounding culture. They were preachers in exile.

In the biblical record, most preachers were voices in the wilderness, not orators in an oasis. Faithful preaching has never depended on a willing audience; it's about preparing people for the coming Christ. We see this clearly in the life of John the Baptist, and his ministry in the desert gives us a positive example of boldness and humility while preaching as exiles.

PREPARING THE WAY

John the Baptizer, as he's sometimes called, appeared after four centuries of silence from God. As the apocryphal book of 1 Maccabees tells us, Israel didn't have a prophetic voice during that time (9:27). No new revelation came to the people of God for 400 years, and then John appeared as "the voice of one crying in the wilderness: 'Prepare the way of the Lord, make his paths straight'" (Mark 1:3).

John paved the way for Christ by calling Israel to repentance. He didn't preach only to common people but to everyone, including religious and political leaders

(Matt. 3:7). Imagine what the Pharisees and Sadducees must have thought of this new preacher, an audacious outsider ministering at the Jordan River. We're told John was there offering a baptism of repentance for the forgiveness of sins. But why should God's people need to be baptized, let alone repent?

In his preaching, John was particularly stern with the Pharisees and the Sadducees, those he called a "brood of vipers" (vv. 7–8). Such preaching required courage. Where did this courage come from? I believe John had two primary motivations: he understood Israel to be under God's judgment and himself to be under God's commission.

This prophet of God knew the urgency of Israel's repentance, realizing it wasn't enough to be a child of Abraham to be saved (vv. 8–9). Hebrew blood didn't provide spiritual immunity. Salvation was secured then only by trusting in the Christ who was to come (Hab. 2:4) and now, for us, by trusting in the Christ who's already come (Rom. 1:17).

Yet I don't think John was a prophet of doom. He was a godly man sensitive to sin. We can see this in his encounter with Herod. At the risk of his life, John confronted the wicked ruler, consistently calling Herod to turn from his unlawful marriage (Mark 6:18). This faithful preaching led to John's arrest, imprisonment, and eventual beheading.

Whether it was to pious Pharisees or corrupt kings, John's approach was the same: He spoke the truth. He called sinners to repentance. Why? Because he was filled with reverence for God and concern for sinners' final destinies. We need more preachers like this today. John wasn't trying to entertain. He was willing to be unpopular. He'd rather see people sorrowful for a moment but joyful for eternity.

Unsurprisingly, John's preaching wasn't well received, either by religious leaders or political powers. If we're also going to be preachers in exile, we must expect similar opposition. We may not see significant results, but our primary calling has never been humanly defined success. The heroes of faith listed in Hebrews 11 bear witness to this truth. Preachers must remain faithful whether people listen or not (cf. Ezek. 2:5).

John preached in the wilderness. That dry land perhaps symbolizes the barren heart of Israel at the time. And who's going to listen to a preacher in the desert of unbelief? For that matter, who's going to listen to us when we preach as exiles in a society that despises Christians and disregards God's Word? No one will listen unless the Spirit draws and convicts him. But the barren desert was where the Spirit led this prophet to preach. And it's the desert—the place we might least expect God to work—where the Spirit often does his greatest miracles.

JOHN'S FORERUNNERS

As John began to preach in the wilderness, we're told he ate locusts and wild honey (Matt. 3:4). This is an insufficient diet for any human. Perhaps this detail reveals not only John's poverty and simplicity but also that he was sustained by God. Like the prophet Elijah, he depended entirely on God for his provision.

John dressed in camel's hair with a leather belt around his waist (Matt. 3:4; Mark 1:6). This was likely an intentional decision to pattern his ministry after Elijah's (2 Kings 1:8). We learn John's commission from God was like Elijah's too: John was to go before Christ "in the spirit and power of Elijah, to turn the hearts of the fathers to the children, and the disobedient to the wisdom of the just, to make ready for the Lord a people prepared" (Luke 1:17).

But John doesn't only follow in the footsteps of Elijah. As Jesus pointed out on multiple occasions, the prophets of old were repeatedly rejected by their hearers (Matt. 5:12; 21:33–36; 23:29–31). God's prophets have often been called to minister in hard places. That was the case for Daniel and Ezekiel, prophets who lived for decades under pagan kings in Babylon.

Ezekiel was sent to speak to the people in exile (Ezek. 1:1), to those who were there because they transgressed God's law for centuries (2:1–7). From the very beginning, Ezekiel was informed about the kind of ministry he'd have: "The house of Israel will not be willing to listen to you, for they are not willing to listen to me: because all the house of Israel have a hard forehead and a stubborn heart" (3:7).

A couple hundred years earlier, the prophet Isaiah was sent to preach to the southern kingdom of Judah. At his calling, Isaiah was informed he'd similarly be unsuccessful (Isa. 6:8–13). Many of the prophets experienced metaphorical exile while living in Israel. Their own people rejected both the prophets and the God who sent them. Israel didn't want their preaching, their counsel, or their warnings. But then again, Jesus said prophets shouldn't expect honor and respect in their hometowns (Mark 6:4).

And so, these preachers were exiles. Estranged from the world, they were never at home. Instead, they were mistreated, persecuted, and even killed (Matt. 23:31). This is the pattern for all who announce God's Word to the world—whether pastors or missionaries, schoolteachers or factory workers, health care providers or delivery drivers. God's spokespeople have often found themselves ostracized and opposed by those they seek to save. They've been preachers in exile.

VOICES IN THE WILDERNESS

Three years ago, the world awoke to a global pandemic. Within weeks, nearly every nation was in lockdown. Airports, seaports, businesses, schools, government offices, and many other facilities were closed. Pastors immediately faced monumental challenges. Were we going to close our church doors? If so, how could we effectively minister to people in the middle of pain and confusion while not in close proximity?

Like many others, I felt the burden to preach. I wanted to comfort and encourage our people while offering them a sense of hope. Meanwhile, many of our people wanted to get back to normal as soon as possible. And yet, when it came to the life of the church, the previous "normal" was part of the problem. In many places throughout Latin America and beyond, the spiritual life of believers diminished significantly. In other places, it almost died.

In those early days, our pastoral team decided to continue our preaching services, which meant speaking to a mostly empty room, to a camera and a group of 10 people in an auditorium that could fit 2,500 people. I remember beginning my message on the first Sunday by stating this was probably the hardest sermon I'd ever preached. I felt compelled to bring consolation and hope to the people watching online. But I was equally compelled to confront those whose lives were lukewarm, not only in our church but also in many other places in Latin America. I was keenly aware our services were being followed in many nations by members of churches that were totally shut down.

So I preached a new series called "Come Back to Me." During that time, I spoke about how to respond when you don't know what to do (2 Chron. 20:12), how to repent and return to God (Jer. 3:12–15), how to have faith in the middle of confusion (Hab. 1–3), and how to renew our worship (Mal. 1–2). By his grace, God used those sermons and others in the series to confront and comfort his people. To remind them, like John, that Christ is coming. To call them to repent.

When the Christian life becomes "church as usual," it's time for the desert. We saw God use the pandemic to prune the church of its superficiality, to strengthen its faith, and to purify its doctrine. If more difficult days are ahead, we must continue to preach in the wilderness. We must not lose heart. We must remember the arid desert can be the place of God's most dramatic work. To be prepared for such a day, we must pay attention to John the Baptist's character. He has much to teach us.

LEARNING FROM JOHN

Jesus said of John, "Among those born of women there has arisen no one greater than John the Baptist" (Matt. 11:11). Yet John was a humble man. He prepared the way then got out of the way. He knew Jesus was the Bridegroom; he was only the friend, the one with short-lived renown. For that reason, John said, "He must increase, but I must decrease" (John 3:29–30). John recognized himself as only an unworthy servant (Luke 3:16).

It can be said John was the only preacher who raised a congregation to follow another preacher (John 1:35–37). That was his purpose. He wasn't jealous of the new rabbi in town. John came to introduce Jesus to the people and then to disappear from their sight. Pastors, if our congregations follow us as leaders, we must follow Christ along with them, pointing them to the chief Shepherd (1 Pet. 5:1–5) so they'll follow him long after we're gone.

Like John, preachers in the wilderness must always remember who we are and who we're not. John knew he wasn't the Messiah. When asked if he was Elijah or the Prophet to come, he answered in the negative. When pressed ("What do you say about yourself?"), he said, "I am the voice of one crying out in the wilderness, 'Make straight the way of the Lord,'" (John 1:20–23). That's all he was, and it's all we can claim to be. Preachers in exile. Voices in the wilderness.

John has always impressed me. But the older I get, the more I appreciate his meekness. John could've said, "I'm the son of Zechariah the priest and a descendant of Aaron, the brother of Moses." He could've introduced himself as the one filled with the Spirit at birth. But John wouldn't say such a thing, because he understood the greatness of a man doesn't consist in what he says about himself but in what he doesn't say. Jesus said John was the greatest person ever born of woman (Matt. 11:11). Yet his greatness was seen in his willingness to take the lowest place (cf. Luke 14:10).

Jesus also identified John as "a burning and shining lamp" and said people "were willing to rejoice for a while in his light" (John 5:35). It seems John experienced some popularity—with crowds following him all the way into the wilderness—but only for a time. Once they came close enough to the lamp to feel the heat, it was too much to bear. Then many left him. Even Herod enjoyed listening to John for a while, but that changed when John confronted him about his sin (Mark 6:17–29).

If cultural exile is on the horizon for the church, preachers might expect a similar response. Churches once full may soon become empty. Instead of willing audiences, we may speak before hostile crowds. As Jesus promised, we may even be taken in to stand before committees, councils, or Congress (13:9). But, as John shows us, even that will be an opportunity for the gospel.

The one who came to prepare the way for the coming Christ never compromised the truth. He never failed to fulfill his responsibility. He preached with boldness and conviction. Like the prophets of old, he acted as the conscience of the nation. And like many of them, he risked his life—eventually losing it. The voice in the wilderness wasn't willing to stay silent to save his skin. He wasn't afraid of dying because he'd already given his life to the One who had called him to preach.

FAITHFUL PREACHERS

Preaching as exiles is a monumental responsibility. At the same time, it's a tremendous privilege. To be God's mouthpiece isn't something we earn or deserve. We didn't apply for the job. We were graciously and sovereignly selected to be God's ambassadors. An ambassador is one sent to another country to bring a message not his own. As Christ's representatives, we must faithfully deliver the message he's entrusted to us (2 Cor. 5:20).

Therefore, we implore others on behalf of Christ to be reconciled to God. We preach the gospel of the One who "made him to be sin who knew no sin, so that in him we might become the righteousness of God" (v. 21). That's our message, the message we must preach whether people listen or not. They need to know "that Christ died for our sins in accordance with the Scriptures, that he was buried, that he was raised on the third day in accordance with the Scriptures" (1 Cor. 15:3–4). Why? Because "we must all appear before the judgment seat of Christ, so that each one may receive what is due for what he has done in the body, whether good or evil" (2 Cor. 5:10).

People must hear the gospel, for there is no salvation unless they call on Christ. But how will they believe in him unless a preacher is sent to them (Rom. 10:14–15)? We are those preachers. We're sent out so the nations might believe and be saved. As we go, let's not forget we must embody this message. Like John, we should be humble, simple, courageous, Christ-centered, submissive, and single-minded. Like John, we should be risk takers, willing to live and serve in hard places, conscious that our lives are not our own.

As exile encroaches, preachers of the gospel must not be like those who shrink back but like those who persevere to the end, encouraging others to do the same for the glory of God. What a glorious race to run and worthy battle to fight! May God find us faithful, proclaiming the truth and calling all people to repent of their sin and trust in the coming King.

CHAPTER 10

APOLOGETICS AS EXILES

Claude Atcho

"Come, see a man who told me all that I ever did. Can this be the Christ?" (John 4:29)

WHEN WAS THE LAST time you heard the Samaritan woman at the well presented as a model for anything, let alone apologetics? I'm guessing the answer is not lately, if ever. Yet there may be no better model of witness in the Gospels than her.

Most teaching about the Samaritan woman centers on her past rather than her preaching. Interpretations of her encounter with Jesus easily focus on speculation, presuming her scandalous past as a prostitute or adulteress. But speculation can be blinding. It can obscure what's explicit in John's narrative: her witness led to a city-wide harvest (John 4:30–42). The Samaritan woman led more people to Christ in a day than most of us will in a lifetime. This shouldn't shame us but instead encourage us to learn from her as a powerful example of apologetics in exile.

Exile is both a theological and a lived reality, one the world has known since Adam plunged humanity into sin and ruin, separating us from fellowship with our Creator. But we can also experience a lesser form of exile, cultural exile, when we're ostracized or opposed by others. Just as Daniel lived in a Babylonian society opposed to the ways of God, so too the church today faces cultural exile. In such a context, Christians and the gospel message are viewed with deep skepticism or outright hostility.

In one sense, these conditions don't matter; the task of Christian witness remains the same. Christians in exile aren't meant simply to survive or retreat but to proclaim the gospel. On the other hand, we can't ignore the deep cultural shifts in the West that have left Christianity distasteful and implausible to many. Recognizing these challenges, Joshua Chatraw writes, "People have so many misunderstandings, critiques, and fears about Christianity, it's hard to even know where to begin."[1]

What if we began with a woman who was herself misunderstood and on the fringes of society, living as a cultural exile? As we'll see, her transforming encounter with Jesus at the well became a powerful apologetic of hope and joy in her community.

---

1. Joshua D. Chatraw, *Telling a Better Story: How to Talk about God in a Skeptical Age* (Grand Rapids, MI: Zondervan, 2020), 9.

APOLOGETICS BEGINS WITH JESUS

When Jesus meets the Samaritan woman, she's alone at the well in the middle of the day. Why did she show up at the hottest time of day? We can't be sure, but she was probably avoiding the townsfolk who treated her with disdain. As Jesus gently reveals, she had five previous husbands and was likely viewed as a person of ill repute.

Whether her succession of marriages was the result of divorce, death, adultery, or a mix of these, we can't know for certain. We do know the Samaritan woman had weathered the hard winds of pain, sin, and suffering. She knew the effects of exile. But when Jesus greets her, by his presence he shifts the trajectory of her whole life toward God's astounding love.

John's narrative demonstrates the power of this encounter first through the deep significance of its setting—it all happens at a well. Multiple biblical patriarchs (or their messengers) met their future brides at a well in a foreign land. Those women often returned home to their families and towns with the good news of their encounters (Gen. 24:28; 29:12; Ex. 2:18–19). John boldly presents Jesus as the true Bridegroom who comes to an unfaithful, scandalized woman at a well in a foreign place and meets her with saving grace, bringing her into fellowship with God "in spirit and truth" (John 4:24). This is a picture of our salvation.

John shows Jesus crossing boundaries to meet this woman. While they're alone at the well, Jesus speaks to her, which crosses two cultural fault lines: her gender as a woman and his as a man, and her ethnicity as Samaritan and his as a Jew. Samaritans believed themselves to be true worshipers of the God of Abraham, but Jews saw them as heretical half-breeds. To call the groups divided would earn you a doctoral degree in understatement. The hostility ran deep. And the hate flowed in both directions (Luke 9:51–54). But Jesus was different. To this Samaritan woman, Jesus speaks, and he even enters her state: he too is thirsty.

As Jesus moved toward her in mercy, the Samaritan woman received him as the long-awaited Messiah. It's easy for Christians to become familiar with this movement of grace. In our brokenness, Jesus knows us and seeks us. With the cultural winds blowing fiercely against us, we must not lose this Christian instinct of mercy. Jesus dignified the Samaritan woman in deep conversation, showing her his love.

This encounter with Jesus then leads to her daring apologetic: "Come, see a man who told me all that I ever did. Can this be the Christ?" (John 4:29). Such bold, public proclamation would be unorthodox for a first-century woman, let alone a woman likely maligned by her neighbors. The bold witness of the Samaritan woman teaches us a truth sometimes deemed too simplistic: the key to apologetics isn't pithy answers or irrefutable arguments but a sense of awe in Jesus that can't be silenced.

APOLOGETICS AND EXPOSURE

Encounters with Jesus bring not only dignity and mercy but also exposure. Painful as it may be, we know such exposure is a subset of divine mercy. Like a doctor who doesn't downplay our diagnosis, Jesus reveals our brokenness and sin for the express purpose of forgiving and healing us. How exposed did the Samaritan woman feel when Jesus revealed his knowledge of her deep secrets? John 4:16–17 captures the moment:

> Jesus said to her, "Go, call your husband, and come here." The woman answered him, "I have no husband." Jesus said to her, "You are right in saying, 'I have no husband'; for you have had five husbands, and the one you now have is not your husband. What you have said is true."

Whatever the reasons for her serial marriages, the point of exposure stands, as does the fact that Jesus declares the man she's with now is *not* her husband (v. 18). Jesus gazes deep into her heart and history. Then he brings her wounds and transgressions into his merciful light.

Will we let Jesus gaze upon us in this way? You can't be a witness apart from such mercy, and you can't experience grace apart from such vulnerability. The result of Christ's merciful exposure isn't condemnation but conversation on the nature of salvation (vv. 19–24). Jesus leads this woman to the growing comprehension that he's the Messiah whom both Jews and Samaritans await

(vv. 25–26), culminating in conversion for the woman and for the many who hear her apologetic appeal (v. 39). It's Christ's mercy through his exposure of her sin that leads her to grasp his identity as Savior. The result isn't fear but joyful excitement. She leaves her water jar and rushes to invite the town to come see Jesus.

In a brokenhearted world, G. K. Chesterton reminded God's people that "joy . . . is the gigantic secret of the Christian."[2] Considering the Samaritan woman as a practitioner of faithful apologetics, I might suggest a remix to Chesterton's maxim: joy is the gigantic secret of the Christian apologetic. The early church father John Chrysostom described the source of the Samaritan woman's powerful witness this way: "Excited by joy, she performed the work of the evangelists."[3] Her encounter with Jesus, in which his truth and grace became real to her, empowered her to become his witness, a joyful laborer in the harvest. Where shame once silenced her voice, gospel joy unleashed it.

AUTHENTICITY IN A SKEPTICAL AGE

In our age, there's little room for *the* truth but ample space for *my* truth. This shift hasn't resulted in the

2. G. K. Chesterton, *Orthodoxy* (Peabody, MA: Hendrickson Publishers, 2006), 155.

3. Robert Louis Wilken, Michael A. Thomas, and Bryan A. Stewart, eds., *John: Interpreted by Early Christian and Medieval Commentators*, trans. Michael A. Thomas and Bryan A. Stewart (Grand Rapids, MI: Eerdmans, 2018), 140.

removal of absolutes but their relocation. Truth is now a matter of authenticity. Truth isn't found outside us; it comes from within when we express what seems good to us. Such a view is troubling and ultimately damaging. But Christians, especially those ready to learn from the Samaritan woman, need not panic. For when societies begin to abandon objective truth and enshrine subjective authenticity, Christians still have something to say. Because Jesus is both objectively true *and* personally real.

To do apologetics faithfully and fruitfully in this cultural moment requires Christians to remember both the objective and personal aspects of our faith. When cultures and societies or friends and family enshrine authenticity, we can speak from our authentic experience of the One who is Truth and Grace for us each day (John 1:14). Peter calls exiles to evangelize through the exaltation of the One who called them from darkness to light (1 Pet. 2:9). This is the sort of apologetic needed in exile: a witness who speaks the objective and subjective reality of God's saving power.

The Samaritan woman is a stellar model of this exilic exaltation. Her witness is potent and simple: "Come, see a man who told *me* all that *I* ever did" (John 4:29). This is her personal experience. It's authentic and rooted in awe. Hers is a testimony that cannot be refuted: a man told me all I ever did. Not only is it *the* truth, but it's also *her* truth. Christians must speak both. In hostile situations or skeptical relationships, we should start with the angle of authenticity: *Let me tell you what Jesus has done, and is doing, in, to, and for me.*

In an age where non-Christians are deeply skeptical of Christianity's goodness and trueness, our apologetics should have this Me-You shape. We can connect people to Christ by telling them what he's done in our lives, calling them to consider what he can do in theirs. Like the Samaritan woman, we'd be wise to major in the language of personal experience birthed from fresh encounters with Jesus, the type of encounters that leave our voices quaking with tremors of hope, surprise, humility, and awe.

This Me-You shape of the Samaritan woman's apologetics is a bit like the floors of a home. Unless you have some sort of superhuman leaping ability, you enter a house on the first floor *then* take the stairs to the second floor. Speaking the truth of our encounters with Jesus is like inviting people into the first floor of a home. "Come, see a man who told me all that I ever did" is incarnational testimony; it's the truth of Jesus manifested in the life of a human. It's the proclamation of why Jesus matters and how the gospel is good, true, and meaningful. Sometimes we get the miracle of starting on the second floor—a friend asks, "Tell me again why you think Christianity is so good?" Or as in Paul's case, someone asks, "What must I do to be saved?" But the first floor is first for a reason; things usually start at step one.

There are several challenges to this type of apologetics. This "first-floor testimony" or a Me-You-shaped apologetic requires vital and ongoing dependence on Jesus. Pride is the great barrier here. This type of apologetics is inescapably personal, which means it's inescapably vulnerable. The Samaritan woman's testimony about Jesus is simultaneously self-incrimination and Christ-exaltation: "Come, see this Jesus! You know all the problems, sins, and rumors of my life? He knew it all, embraced me still, and made himself known to me!" To say, "He told me all I ever did" is to put your moral business out there for all to see.

To learn from the model of the Samaritan woman, our apologetics must be tinged with the flavor of humiliation, with the willingness to say, "Here's the difference Jesus makes in my life. Because apart from his healing grace, I have flaws, needs, and sins that might make your face turn red." This way of apologetics means the crucifixion of our performative personas so we can exalt the crucified Savior who redeems and transforms our lives.

Several years ago, while in graduate school, a close friend of mine agreed to read with me Tim Keller's apologetic classic *The Reason for God*. I was thrilled and hopeful. As we discussed the book, we had some good conversations. Then the topic turned to grace, and my friend mentioned he and I didn't need forgiveness as much as *some people*.

I felt the air in the room thicken. In my heart, I knew I needed in that moment to move from vague Christian generalities—"I'm a sinner"—to real-world particulars. I needed to tell him exactly how I've messed things up, exactly how I've hurt people, exactly how I've thought unthinkable thoughts. The moment called for the specifics of my sinfulness in a way that would leave me embarrassed and God's grace exalted. Instead, pride tightened

my throat, and no words came out—except for a few ge-
neric platitudes. Unlike the Samaritan woman, I couldn't
point to the "all I ever did" nature of my brokenness. I
spoke the truth generically rather than flavoring it with
my truth specifically, and my witness suffered.

EMBRACE AN APOLOGETIC SPIRITUALITY

When we follow the pattern of witness presented by the
Samaritan woman, we embrace an apologetic spirituality
imbued with the joy, humility, and authenticity of encountering Jesus. These personal experiences with the living Christ fuel us to point others to him. In directing our
friends and family to Christ, we're implicitly calling them
to consider him, inviting them up the stairs to the second
floor. We're joining the Samaritan woman in her broad-
casted command to "Come, and see." Her invitation is an
echo of Jesus's call to the first disciples (John 1:39), which
they imitate in calling others to follow Christ (v. 46). By
issuing a joyful, first-floor invitation to consider Jesus, we
stand in the apologetic tradition of the first disciples and
of our Lord himself.

The second step of the Samaritan woman's witness
ventures from a personal testimony to its all-encompassing
implication: "Can this be the Christ?" (4:29). We too can
make the turn from "my truth" and its Me-You shape to
helping others consider "the Truth," a Me-You-Christ
movement. This movement to the second floor happens
through open questions that follow on the heels of our
spoken experience of Jesus. When I share with a friend

how through prayer Christ is helping me endure a brutal stretch of work, I can add a question that not only leaves my friend interested in my experience but invites him to consider his relationship to the truth that has shaped me: "Have you ever thought if God might help you with your problem?" or "Would you ever be open to learning to pray as Jesus taught?" Such questions present the reality of Christ to our friends, offering them a simple way to "take a step" toward the truth of the gospel. This allows them to "come and see" on the journey to trusting and believing.

There are two levels to the Samaritan woman's apologetic witness, and the order matters. In a skeptical age, many will close themselves off from Christ, humanly speaking, apart from an authentic gospel witness from a trusted friend. Thus we must often start at the first floor. This doesn't mean we always slow-play the call for others to consider Christ, only that we recognize the importance of a personal apologetic as a starting place. But just as there are two levels to our witness, there are also two levels to people's responses. Those we witness to must not only believe our experience but venture on to embrace Christ themselves. Initially, the Samaritans believe because of the woman's authentic, joyful, and vulnerable testimony (v. 39). Then they ultimately believe for themselves from their own encounters with Jesus (v. 42). What begins at the first floor ends at the second; what starts with a joyful testimony ends in the joy of salvation.

When we speak of what Jesus is doing in us, it opens the door for people to consider Jesus for themselves. This isn't argumentative apologetics; it's an apologetic spirituality rooted in encountering Christ. Our witness, our apologetics, will have no pulse and no power apart from a life-giving experience with Christ that shapes us day after day. This is what we learn from the woman who came to the well an exile, encountered Life, and with great joy spoke of being known and loved.

CHAPTER 11

VOCATION AS EXILES

Jay Y. Kim

"But seek the welfare of the city where I have sent you into exile, and pray to the LORD on its behalf, for in its welfare you will find your welfare." (Jer. 29:7)

DURING MOST OF MY college years, I worked part-time at a bank. I started as a teller before eventually becoming an assistant branch manager. The job paid well, especially for a young college kid, and was straightforward. It was the sort of work that was easy to leave behind when the workday ended. But as many do in their early 20s, I became increasingly discontent. The job was fine, but it wasn't meaningful. It didn't satisfy my growing need for purpose and significance.

A job is necessary, but what most people are seeking is *vocation*—their *voice* (from which the word is derived) into the world, their unique contribution to the ongoing conversation of human history. The ability to potentially "disrupt the industry" always begins with the angst of "What should I do with my life?"—an expression of vocational longing. But the question is somewhat misleading. Tim Keller writes, "A job is a vocation only if someone else calls you to do it and you do it for them rather than for yourself."[1] Vocational calling isn't found within; we receive it from another. Vocation is a gift given, not a treasure hidden.

In her essay titled "Why Work?," Dorothy Sayers quotes the French philosopher Jacques Maritain and writes, "If you want to produce Christian work, be a Christian, and try to make a work of beauty into which you have put your heart; do not adopt a Christian pose."[2] Vocation is the calling to serve others by creating a heartfelt work of beauty. An artist's painting, an engineer's code, a teacher's lesson, a baker's cake, a stay-at-home parent's myriad of responsibilities—these and so much more are vocation, the gift of invitation to offer our best effort, to God's glory and for the good of others, in the various places and spaces we occupy.

Living in exile on this side of eternity, the gift of vocation, when received gratefully and stewarded responsibly, offers immense hope and opportunity for followers of Jesus. Vocation offers us a chance to truly disrupt

1.   Timothy Keller, *Every Good Endeavor: Connecting Your Work to God's Work* (New York: Penguin Books, 2012), 2.

2.   Dorothy Sayers, "Why Work?," accessed February 10, 2023, https://www1.villanova.edu/content/dam/villanova/mission/faith/Why%20Work%20by%20Dorothy%20Sayers.pdf.

things—not just industries but culture itself. Vocation as exiles calls Christians to disrupt a culture of self-interest with sacrificial, self-giving love by leveraging skills and resources in partnership with others, for God's glory and the good of all.

SETTING UP SHOP IN EXILE

In Acts 18, the apostle Paul makes his way from Athens to Corinth and meets a married couple there, Aquila and Priscilla. Aquila was a Jew from the Roman province of Pontus (in modern Turkey), but many scholars believe Priscilla was from a wealthy, aristocratic Roman family.[3]

Luke tells us the couple had recently relocated from Italy because Emperor Claudius had commanded all the Jews to leave Rome (vv. 1–2). Since she was married to a Jewish man, Priscilla was expelled from her homeland along with her husband. Together they land in Corinth, where they meet Paul. The three of them, brought together by their shared experience as exiles in a land not their own, work together.

Paul, Priscilla, and Aquila were "tentmakers by trade" (v. 3). Because of the itinerant nature of Paul's work, it's unlikely he carried the necessary materials to set up shop and launch an operable tentmaking business of his own in the various places his travels took him. It's far more

3. "The Tentmaker Priscilla (Acts 18:2)," Theology of Work, accessed February 10, 2023, https://www.theologyofwork.org/key-topics/women-workers-in-the-new-testament/the-tentmaker-priscilla-acts-182.

likely he carried a few smaller tools with which he could execute minor repairs. But in Corinth, he partnered with Priscilla and Aquila, who'd established a viable tentmaking business there.

These three exiled followers of Jesus shared their skills and resources, set up shop in a frenetic foreign city, and presumably went about the work of crafting tents for a wide variety of clientele. And in a competitive marketplace like Corinth, it's safe to assume they held their work to a high quality standard. They wouldn't have been in business long otherwise. Finally, as we learn from the broader story of Paul's missionary journeys and Priscilla and Aquila's significant influence on a number of churches throughout the region, tentmaking was simply the exterior of a much deeper, much more meaningful vocational engagement in exile.

FOR THE GOOD OF ALL

At the risk of stating the obvious, Paul, Priscilla, and Aquila didn't make "Christian" tents. They were Christians who made tents for all. Evidence indicates they would've made leather tents.[4] At the time, leather tents were purchased in bulk by the Roman military to house their soldiers during long treks to battle, making them a likely client. This is a fascinating tension for Christians. Does vocation in exile require an ethical compromise?

4.   "The Tentmaker Priscilla."

What does vocation in exile mean for the medical professional when it comes to the sanctity of life? What does it mean for the business owner when it comes to serving customers who uphold values distinctly counter to Scripture? What about for the parent when it comes to juggling her child's schedule between academics, sports, and church?

I recently talked with a friend about the tension she's experiencing as a public school teacher. Faced with mounting pressure to affirm and teach modern cultural mores around sexuality and gender, she's navigating the complex intersection between personal faithfulness and public witness. Her courageous conclusion was that the two are one and the same. The most loving thing she could offer her students, their families, and her fellow faculty was a loving, resilient, and kind but firm commitment to what she believed to be true, while also leaving enough room for meaningful dialogue with those who disagree with her position.

Vocation in exile necessitates clarity and conviction coupled with empathy and compassion. Ultimately, there's no vocation, no human endeavor, that works toward God's glory and the true common good while also directly violating God's plan for his glory and our good. This would be an untenable incongruity. Navigating the tension of vocation in exile involves a loving sensitivity and some amount of nuance but must always remain anchored in God's vision for human flourishing, unswayed by cultural tides. Embodying and expressing this vision requires courageous, loving resistance. And part of resisting is remaining rather than retreating. This has been God's plan for his people in exile since the earliest days.

Six hundred years before Christ, the people of God lived in Babylonian exile. But they did so under the impression they'd be back home in no time. They expected God to swiftly restore them and return them to their land. But God had other plans, which he voiced through the prophet Jeremiah:

> Thus says the LORD of hosts, the God of Israel, to all the exiles whom I have sent into exile from Jerusalem to Babylon: Build houses and live in them; plant gardens and eat their produce. Take wives and have sons and daughters; take wives for your sons, and give your daughters in marriage, that they may bear sons and daughters; multiply there, and do not decrease. But seek the welfare of the city where I have sent you into exile, and pray to the LORD on its behalf, for in its welfare you will find your welfare. (Jer. 29:4–7)

God instructed the people living in exile to settle in and settle down, to build houses, plant gardens, marry, and raise families. The invitation culminated in a counterintuitive call: "Seek the welfare of the city where I have sent you into exile, and pray to the LORD on its behalf."

The word translated "welfare" in the ESV is the Hebrew word *shalom*, which is most often translated "peace." In the NIV, the phrase is "Seek the peace and prosperity of the city." Vocation in exile is fundamentally incongruous with and paradoxical to the standard approach in culture today, where the goal for many is to get in, get rich, and get out. Christians are called to settle in and settle down in our current Babylons, to build and plant, to seek the welfare of the city, to work toward the peace and prosperity of all within proximal reach.

Joseph de Veuster was born in rural Belgium in 1840. In his late teens, he felt a call to ministry. At age 23, he left for the Hawaiian Islands as a missionary. Upon arrival, Veuster learned that lepers in Hawaii were deported to an island called Molokai and discarded to live as exiles. Heartbroken and moved to compassion, Veuster volunteered to live with, serve, and love the lepers of Molokai. He took the religious name Damien and spent the rest of his life pastoring in Molokai until he himself contracted leprosy, eventually leading to his death before his 50th birthday. Today, we know him as Father Damien of Molokai, because he settled in, built houses, planted gardens, and worked for the good of all in Jesus's name. This is what vocation in exile looks like.

SPIRIT-FILLED ARTISTRY

Priscilla and Aquila helped establish Christian churches almost everywhere they went (cf. Acts 18:26; Rom. 16:3–5; 1 Cor. 16:19). They were also financial patrons of Paul's missionary works.[5] All of this required financial means. Priscilla likely came from an affluent family, but the consistent and continuous nature of Priscilla and Aquila's generosity toward the early Christian church and Paul's missionary work over many years implies their tentmaking business was profitable, perhaps significantly so. Tentmaking was a fairly common and competitive industry in the first-century world. Profitability required quality. Aquila and Priscilla made quality tents.

Paul affirms this value of skilled work when he says, "In all things I have shown you that by working hard in this way we must help the weak and remember the words of the Lord Jesus, how he himself said, 'It is more blessed to give than to receive'" (Acts 20:35). He also writes, "Work with your hands, as we instructed you, so that you may walk properly before outsiders and be dependent on no one" (1 Thess. 4:11–12). In the words of one scholar, Aquila and Priscilla, along with Paul, were "established artisans" of tentmaking.[6]

The difference between a job and a vocation often comes down to artisanship. For some, work is a matter of function. It's primarily transactional: "If I do X, I will get Y." Bare minimum in this case is both acceptable

5.   Justin Taylor, "What the Tentmaking Business Was Really Like for the Apostle Paul," The Gospel Coalition, June 26, 2020, https://www. thegospelcoalition.org/blogs/justin-taylor/what-the-tentmaking-business-was-really-like-for-the-apostle-paul/.
6.   Kenneth Berding, "Was Paul a Tentmaker? Part 1: Did Paul Make Literal Tents?," The Good Book Blog, October 18, 2021, https://www. biola.edu/blogs/good-book-blog/2021/was-paul-a-tentmaker-part-1-did-paul-make-literal-tents.

and a strategically sound approach. But the artisan cares less about transactional functionality and far more about quality, beauty, and the loving expression of skill. The true artisan cares about these things not for the sake of self-glorification but for the simple and profound joy of offering the world something of value.

In the ancient exodus story, as God leads his people through the wilderness, he calls a man named Bezalel to lead the effort to build the tent of meeting, the ark, and all their furnishings—the physical space and surroundings of the intersection between heaven and earth. God says of this artisan, "I have filled him with the Spirit of God, with ability and intelligence, with knowledge and all craftsmanship, to devise artistic designs" (Ex. 31:3–4). Of course, for who could create something of such majestic and divine proportions without the divine skill given by God himself?

Vocation in exile is Spirit-filled artistry carried out by sanctified artisans. Whether teaching, engineering, stay-at-home parenting, manual labor, finance, or any other work, Christians are called to do quality work, not just for the sake of profitability but primarily to bear witness to the God who fills us with ability, intelligence, knowledge, and all craftsmanship. Such work has the potential to create faint glimpses of heaven on earth, home in exile. The vocational gift we receive in exile is meant to express beauty and skill. To an unbelieving world languishing in the toil of transactional work, it should spark curiosity toward the possibility of something more, something holy. As such, Christian vocation is truly disruptive to the culture.

SOUL WORK

In his letter to the Colossian church, Paul writes, "Whatever you do, work heartily, as for the Lord and not for men" (Col. 3:23). He writes broadly to all the early Christians in Colossae, but, notably, the verse preceding this instruction is addressed specifically to "bondservants," from the Greek word *douloi*, which is often translated as "slaves."

Slavery in the first-century Greco-Roman world wasn't what we most often think of today when we hear the word, namely, the transatlantic slave trade. "Bondservants" is indeed a good translation. In Paul's day, slavery was a viable and common option for making a living. By some estimates, between 30 and 50 percent of the population in the first century was made up of those who'd sold themselves into servitude, often to pay a debt or escape poverty. At the time, slavery, or becoming a bondservant, was not race-based.

Paul had a wealthy friend in Colossae named Philemon, after whom another New Testament letter is named. In that letter, Paul entreats Philemon to receive back a man named Onesimus: "[Have him back] no longer as a bondservant but more than a bondservant, as a beloved brother. . . . So if you consider me your partner, receive him as you would receive me" (Philem. 16–17). Onesimus had once been a slave in Philemon's household. Reading between the lines of the text in both Colossians and Philemon, Onesimus had likely wronged his master in some way, possibly by stealing money, and had fled into exile. He eventually meets Paul and becomes a Christian. Now, Paul is sending Onesimus back to his former master. But he does so by leveling the playing field. They're no longer master and slave but beloved brothers.

With the complexity and tension of this tenuous relationship lingering, Paul writes to all involved and to bondservants in particular, "Whatever you do, work heartily, as for the Lord and not for men" (Col. 3:23). The word "heartily" in the Greek is the word *psyches*, coming from the root word most often translated "soul." Whatever we do, in all we do, followers of Jesus are called to soul work, regardless of rank, responsibility, or position. Masters and bondservants; upper management, middle managers, and the general workforce; white collar, blue collar, and no collar; artists and artisans; stay-at-home parents and teachers—if you're a Christian, your vocation is a calling to bare your soul, to lay it down before God as a labor of love.

SUBWAY SYMPHONY

On January 12, 2007, Joshua Bell stood at the entrance of the L'Enfant Plaza metro station in Washington, DC, and played his violin. He played for 43 minutes. In that time, more than a thousand people passed him by, but only seven stopped to listen for any length of time. A handful more dropped some change out of courtesy. In all, Joshua Bell made $32 that day. A few days before, he'd sold out Symphony Hall in Boston, with most tickets going for more than $100 each. The violin he played that busy Friday morning in Washington, DC, was his Stradivarius, valued at more than $3 million. And hardly anyone noticed.

This now well-known social experiment has often been cited in the years since as evidence of society's sad inability to recognize true artistry, or the manifestation of the frenzied chaos of a culture constantly on the go, or any number of other cultural ills. But I think all of these miss the point, and the beauty, of the experiment. For 43 minutes on a Friday morning in a busy metro, the ordinary became extraordinary as a musician offered his gift. As brilliance overtook the mundane sounds of busy footsteps and trains, vocation was unfolding, Joshua Bell's unique voice spoke into the world through his violin. Whether people noticed or not was secondary. The fact remains, something remarkable happened that day.

As Christians, vocation as exiles is like a subway symphony. Wherever we are, no matter how ordinary or mundane or ill-fitting or unappreciative the environment may be, we set up shop, bare our souls unto the Lord, lean into Spirit-filled artistry, and offer the gift of vocation we've received back out into the world as a gift for all, for the good of all, and for the glory of God.

CHAPTER 12

CHURCH AS EXILES

Alex Duke

"Let us hold fast the confession of our hope without wavering, for he who promised is faithful. And let us consider how to stir up one another to love and good works, not neglecting to meet together, as is the habit of some, but encouraging one another, and all the more as you see the Day drawing near." (Heb. 10:23–25)

MY FAMILY AND I lived for two years as one of the few white families in Flushing, New York. We miss a lot of things about New York City—Saturday afternoons in Central or Domino Park, Friday nights at The Landmark of 57th West, and Arthur Ashe Kids' Day before the U.S. Open. But what we miss most is the food. From Korean BBQ to Chinese hot pot to halal trucks to the endless variety of New York–style pizza, nothing compares to the food scene in Queens.

I suppose part of the reason is that New York City is full of exiles. Almost everyone's from somewhere else, even if they've lived in Queens all their lives. They're between two homes—the one they've known and the one their parents or grandparents used to know. In the best of situations, this reality creates culturally conversant and adaptable kids; it's wonderful. In the worst of situations, it creates kids who don't speak the same language as their parents, kids who feel most alone when they're at home with their families.

The comparison isn't exact, but healthy local churches are full of people between two homes. They're exiles. But whereas kids in NYC live between the present and the past, our tension runs in the opposite direction. We live between the present and the future, between the home we grew up in and the home we're heading toward. It's why the "exile" metaphor is so apt for Christians. And it's both wonderful and tragic.

For Christians, our unavoidable immersion in the present can dull our longing for the future, tempting us to merely blend into a world we're supposed to bless. Thankfully, our God knows this, so he gave us the local church, where we gather each week to feast on the glorious promises of the gospel. Through our local churches, we receive instruction from the Word that reinterprets our past, fuels us for the present, and shifts our ultimate hope toward the future Christ has already secured for us.[1]

1. This is effectively the argument made in Heb. 10:23–25.

Christians may read that sentence and say "Amen" while having no idea how the abstract encouragement moves to actual reality. The goal of this chapter is to help make that connection explicit. In particular, we'll reflect on the life and work of Timothy as both a Christian and a pastor, as both a model exile and a model leader of exiles.

FIGHTING FOR FAITH

Timothy was the son of an unbelieving Greek father and a believing Jewish mother (Acts 16:1, 3)—so he likely knew what it was to live between two worlds. His mother, Eunice, and his grandmother, Lois, passed down their "sincere faith" to him from a young age (2 Tim. 1:5). Sometime after his conversion, he accompanied Paul as his protégé and functioned as his representative to various churches (1 Cor. 4:17; Phil. 2:19). At some point, Timothy was imprisoned and later released (Heb. 13:23).

We also know he served as the pastor of a struggling church in Ephesus. That's why we have 1 and 2 Timothy, Paul's letters to his pastor friend who, amid a disastrous situation, wasn't sure what to do. Paul's solution was to give clear instructions to Timothy for the church but also to encourage him to "share in suffering as a good soldier" (2 Tim. 2:3). Clearly, Paul was concerned his son in the faith may shrink in retreat if the battle continued to rage.[2]

---

2. You should read slowly through 1 and 2 Tim. before finishing this chapter. After all, I'm on a puritanical word count, and I can't afford to quote every reference I make!

Timothy's primary opponents were false teachers. Like clowns who make balloon animals at a child's birthday party, they twisted God's law so it said strange things about genealogies (1 Tim. 1:4), marriage (4:3), and food laws (4:3). Paul explained these men were "swerving from" truth (1:6) as they shipwrecked their faith (1:19); they were "liars" (4:2) who were "puffed up" (6:4) and addicted to controversy (6:4–5). They were also hypocrites. They were "godly" because they were greedy for gain; they loved morality because they loved money (6:5, 9–10).

And those were just the challenges from his first letter! By the time Timothy received the sequel, Paul was at death's door and Timothy's situation seemed more or less unchanged. Interestingly, Paul's counsel *also* seems more or less unchanged.

So what's the divine strategy when the gospel is under attack because false teachers have scaled the church's walls? Do we retreat? Do we capitulate? Do we reframe our beliefs and reposition our posture so the grinding conflict smooths out? Do we accentuate our similarities to our opponents so they see we're not all that different anyway?

In short, no, no, no—and no.

We face similar questions. We live in a world awash in false teaching. We're told it's narrow-minded to believe Jesus is the only way. It's bigoted to believe men and women are created fundamentally different. And it's narrow-minded *and* bigoted to believe a church ought to be led by qualified men called pastors. False teaching is orthodoxy outside the church. We get that. But false teaching can also be a siren song *inside* the church, a magnet for the immature, doubtful, and disaffected.

If I could summarize Paul's counsel to Timothy into a single command, it would be something like this: *Fight for unstained doctrine and unstained living so that at the end of your life, you may receive an unstained crown of glory.* That's the "good warfare" and "good fight" Timothy must commit himself to. That's his job as a pastor. And guess what? It's our job as Christians to enlist ourselves in that work too.

FINDING FAITHFUL CHURCHES

How do we find churches that help us fight for unstained doctrine and unstained living in order to receive our unstained crown? What should we even look for? A few things come to mind.

1. FIND A CHURCH THAT PRIZES DOCTRINE.

Paul exhorted Timothy to wage a war with words as his primary weapons (1 Tim. 4:6, 11, 13–16; 6:2, 13–14, 20; 2 Tim. 1:13, 14; 2:2, 14, 15; 3:14–15; 4:1–2). As we read through 1 and 2 Timothy, it's clear the pastor is both steward and soldier; he always defends the Maginot Line, and he sometimes storms the beaches of Normandy. Though he fundamentally preserves, he also proactively attacks.

A pastor should guard the truth, follow the pattern, continue in the truth, and remind others of what's been passed down to him. How? Primarily by preaching the

Word (2 Tim. 4:2). There's no better foundation than a ministry built on patient and even repetitive proclamation of what God's Word says about God's glorious Son (1 Tim. 1:15–18; 3:16; 6:13–16; 2 Tim. 1:8–10; 2:8).

But guarding isn't *always* defensive. After all, as George Washington once said, sometimes the best defense is a good offense.[3] That's precisely why Paul encourages Timothy to defend truth *and* destroy falsehood (1 Tim. 1:3; 2:8–15; 4:7; 5:1–25; 6:3, 8–10, 20; 2 Tim. 2:23; 3:1–9).

The burden of the pastor and the Christian is to resist the temptation to pick and choose which truths to defend and which falsehoods to destroy. "Don't love money!" happens to be a command from Paul that many will agree with, including the Notorious B.I.G. and adherents to the Quran. But Christians must recognize all Scripture is profitable (2 Tim. 3:16), the parts that make sense in this world and the parts that are otherworldly.

So we'll speak about the danger of greed *and* the danger of not paying our pastors. We'll speak about the dignity of families caring for their own widows *and* the dishonor of women usurping roles God has reserved for men. And we'll challenge men who shamefully retreat when they should step forward.[4]

---

3. Seriously, he did! "Offensive operations, often times, is the *surest*, if not *only* (in some cases) means of defence." George Washington to John Trumbull, letter, June 25, 1799, National Historical Publications and Records Commission, https://founders.archives.gov/documents/Washington/06-04-02-0120.

4. All these topics are covered in 1 and 2 Tim. But, of course, since you did your homework, you already know this!

Christians, then, should seek a church that teaches the whole counsel of God, not weaponizing its words to the "world out there" but also addressing failures within its own walls. As Paul warns Timothy, there's a time coming when people won't endure sound teaching but instead will accumulate teachers who only reinforce what they already believe or want to believe (2 Tim. 4:3–4). Such teachers fail the most basic test of faithfulness. They preside over a church full of yes-men and yes-women rather than exiles.

As usual, there are ditches on both sides of the road to faithfulness. One ditch is for itchy-ear preachers, nonconfrontational accumulators of crowds. Such men (and women) effectively waste their pulpits by leaving lost people without direction and saved people without correction. The other ditch is for opposition-obsessed preachers, overly confrontational accumulators of a different kind of crowd. Such men effectively waste their pulpits by failing to equip exiles to navigate with love and wisdom an increasingly difficult world.

So find a church that cares about doctrine. As you're on the lookout, 1 and 2 Timothy should keep you on the straight and narrow. But there's more to say.

2. FIND A CHURCH THAT PRIZES CHARACTER.

Paul exhorts Timothy time and time again to fight for the truth. But he spends perhaps just as much time exhorting Timothy to be a specific kind of man, and in doing so to become a model for all Christians.

The obvious place to point to is Paul's list of expectations for elders and deacons (1 Tim. 3). But both letters are shot through with similar encouragements about character (1 Tim. 1:5, 12–16; 2:8–12; 4:12, 16; 2 Tim. 2:24–26; 3:10).

Who cares what you *believe* if you can't first *be*? And what kind of person should you be? A loving person with a pure heart and clean conscience. A humble person who's astonished she gets to serve Christ in the first place. An exemplary person who studies himself as much as he studies the Scriptures. A person who fights without being quarrelsome. A person who endures evil and keeps smiling.

While these two values—doctrine and character—may seem distinct, they're interrelated and even interdependent. Consider Paul's opening remarks:

As I urged you when I was going to Macedonia, remain at Ephesus so that you may charge certain persons not to teach any different doctrine, nor to devote themselves to myths and endless genealogies, which promote speculations rather than the stewardship from God that is by faith. The aim of our charge is love that issues from a pure heart and a good conscience and a sincere faith. Certain persons, by swerving from these, have wandered away into vain discussion, desiring to be teachers of the law, without understanding either what they are saying or the things about which they make confident assertions. (1 Tim. 1:3–7)

Did you notice the connection? The error these false teachers made wasn't getting their doctrine from some strange first-century subreddit. Their first misstep was swerving away from love. Their theological error was born out of a moral and motivational error. They *wanted* to be teachers, but they ended up teaching things they didn't understand. They *wanted* to elevate the law and morality, but they tried to produce fruit without the root. Instead, they should have wanted to be teachers because they loved God and others with a sincere faith. And they should have led others to a similar and sincere love. But they failed.

What a tall task for pastors; what a tall task for all Christians.

Like Timothy, we're facing confusing and difficult times. As we live as exiles in a fallen world, we'll be tempted—like these false teachers—to swerve in our teaching and our temperament. We'll be tempted to wonder if our meek and meager faithfulness even matters. In those moments, we need to reorient our perspective and remember Paul's words to Timothy:

> The Lord's servant must not be quarrelsome but kind to everyone, able to teach, patiently enduring evil, correcting his opponents with gentleness. God may perhaps grant them repentance leading to a knowledge of the truth, and they may come to their senses and escape from the snare of the devil, after being captured by him to do his will. (2 Tim. 2:24–26)

Church leaders need to remember we defend the gospel and fight for faith through our gentleness, kindness, patience, respect, and love. We need letters like 1 and 2 Timothy because they hold out to us models of faithful exiles, from Paul and Timothy in particular to the offices of elder and deacon in general. It's a good thing for men and women to want to look like Paul and Timothy, since elders and deacons are models of godly character for the whole church. Does that describe you? Then meditate on Paul's words, and find a church led by those of good character who are worth following.

3. FIND A CHURCH THAT PRIZES OUR HOPE IN A SECURE FUTURE.

The sum total of our church's teaching and our church leaders' temperament subtly but surely shifts our ultimate hope toward our secure future with the Lord Jesus. They remind us we are, in fact, exiles—people from somewhere else, people between two homes.

And yet we're not homeless exiles, because we have the local church. We're members, as Paul says, of "the household of God" (1 Tim. 3:15), the best place on earth to see God's authority on display and our responsibility in action.

How can that be? These metaphors seem to be at odds. They aren't. God in his infinite wisdom has gathered us strangers together and made us siblings. We should feel like exiles *least* when we're gathered with our spiritual family.

That otherworldly truth doubles as a rallying cry for exiles. If we look around our church next Sunday, we'll see lots of people with whom we have many differences—some trivial, some far from it. But if we all can confess this "mystery of godliness" together (v. 16) with a sincere faith and pure conscience, then guess what? We've found a temporary home.

But we haven't yet arrived at our ultimate home. We're still fighting, still running, still waiting for our crown of righteousness we'll receive at his appearing (2 Tim. 4:6–10). Until that day, we must plant roots in a healthy church and give our whole selves to it—for the next 5, 10, or 50 years. We must be shaped and captivated by the gospel that our qualified leaders proclaim and protect.

The church, at its best, is God's appointed means to make us faithful exiles to the very end.

CHAPTER 13

SUFFERING AS EXILES

Blair Linne

"Beloved, I urge you as sojourners and exiles to abstain from the passions of the flesh, which wage war against your soul. Keep your conduct among the Gentiles honorable, so that when they speak against you as evildoers, they may see your good deeds and glorify God on the day of visitation." (1 Pet. 2:11–12)

IF YOU'RE FAMILIAR WITH Peter's story, you might not expect him to be the disciple who'd write the primary letter in the New Testament on suffering. Instead, you could assume he'd write on overcoming pride, finding forgiveness, or the dangers of sinking when taking your eyes off Jesus.

This Galilean fisherman left all to follow Jesus and supernaturally confessed him as the Christ (Matt. 16:16). But when Jesus revealed he was going to suffer and die,

Peter rebuked him. In response, Jesus said, "Get behind me, Satan! You are a hindrance to me. For you are not setting your mind on the things of God, but on the things of man" (v. 23). How awkward is that? Peter got it spectacularly wrong; he failed to understand that the cross was the ordained means for the Suffering Servant to save his people from their sins.

Peter also failed when the time came for him to suffer. When his association with Jesus threatened his life, Peter denied knowing his Lord. Although he was the first disciple to follow Jesus, Peter was also the first genuine disciple to disown Jesus. So how does this man write a letter to Christians who are suffering?

The only explanation is the resurrection. Peter walked into Jesus's hollow tomb, saw the linen clothes, and found his body was gone. Along with the other apostles, Peter was an eyewitness to Jesus's resurrection from the dead. And it was the risen Lord who graciously appeared to Peter, asked him to affirm his love, and gave him the call to feed his sheep (John 21:15–19).

Through Jesus's restoration and the power of the Spirit, Peter matured from the unpredictable firecracker of a disciple we see in the Gospels to the bold rock in the book of Acts who endured persecution. This man who collapsed under the threat of suffering now had courage to stand before authorities and testify to this Jesus whom God raised from the dead (Acts 2:32).

This is the Peter who wrote to believers in Pontus, Galatia, Cappadocia, Asia, and Bithynia (1 Pet. 1:1), encouraging them to endure as elect exiles. He was no longer turned off by the idea of suffering. Since Peter knew believers would face fiery trials, he wanted them—and us—to understand that, as for Christ, suffering isn't where our story ends.

NOT YET HOME

Most commentators believe the audience of 1 Peter to be Gentile Christians. Throughout the letter, he references their former way of living. He writes, "For the time that is past suffices for doing what the Gentiles want to do, living in sensuality, passions, drunkenness, orgies, drinking parties, and lawless idolatry. With respect to this they are surprised when you do not join them in the same flood of debauchery, and they malign you" (4:3–4). This suggests Peter's readers were once part of an idolatrous, unbelieving community. Since their friends are surprised at their lack of participation in debauched practices and idol worship, we assume that prior to regeneration they were living like all the other Gentiles in the empire.

Throughout the letter, Peter employs Jewish motifs to supply these Gentile Christians with a new identity. For example, he starts the letter off by calling them "elect" (1:1) and later "a chosen race, a royal priesthood, a holy nation" (2:9). These same words were spoken during the exodus journey when the Israelites escaped Pharoah (Ex. 19:5–6). By using similar language, Peter connects the identity and experience of these Gentile believers under the evil rule of Rome with Israel in the wilderness having just escaped Pharoah.

He also calls his readers exiles of the dispersion (1 Pet. 1:1). Dispersion or "Diaspora" was a term often used to refer to Jewish people scattered throughout the nations (John 7:35). But it was later used to describe Christians (James 1:1). Again, Peter connects the identity of his Gentile audience with God's people in the old covenant. Like Israel, these exiles were sojourners and strangers, temporary residents far from home.

The life of Olaudah Equiano illustrates what this exile can look like. Equiano was born in Benin in 1745 and authored the first autobiography of an enslaved person. He was stolen in West Africa before being sold to European slavers and sent to the West Indies, eventually ending up in Virginia. Equiano indeed was a stranger in a foreign land. The larceny, land, language, and labor were all unfamiliar. Once Equiano converted to Christianity, he understood what it was to be an exile not only geographically but also spiritually, leading him to write about the blatant hypocrisy of Christians who championed chattel slavery:

O, ye nominal Christians! might not an African ask you, learned you this from your God, who says unto you, Do unto all men as you would men should do unto you? Is it not enough that we are torn from our

country and friends to toil for your luxury and lust
of gain?[1]

Along with many other Africans that were abducted,
sold as chattel, and forced into a life of endless slavery,
Equiano knew what it was to suffer as an exile. While
the circumstances in Peter's day were different, their sufferings were similar.

These Gentile Christians were exiles spiritually. Because of their commitment to Christ and his commands,
they couldn't live with a sense of belonging in their com-
munities. And they were exiles geographically. Perhaps
some were displaced from their physical homes, but all
were strangers on earth and far from heaven.

The suffering these believers faced was extensive.
They endured fiery trials (1 Pet. 4:12–13, 16) and experienced grief (1:6). They suffered with sin and were tempted to return to their former behaviors (2:1–3). They were
insulted (4:14) and intimidated (3:14). They had unbelieving spouses (3:1) and lived under unjust human authorities (2:13–18). On top of that, their adversary the Devil
wanted to devour them (5:8).

Aren't these the types of sufferings we experience
too? Trials of the flesh, the world, and the Devil. But Peter tells them and us not to be shocked when we face
these difficulties (4:12) since we know "the same kinds

---

1.   Olaudah Equiano, *The Interesting Narrative of the Life of Olaudah
     Equiano, Or Gustavus Vassa, The African* (London, 1789; Project
     Gutenberg, 2005), chap. 2, https://www.gutenberg.org/ebooks/15399.

of suffering are being experienced by [our] brotherhood throughout the world" (5:9). All Christians face this suffering. None of us is at home. Instead, we're living in the now-but-not-yet reality of Christ's kingdom. While we do have the hope that when Christ returns we'll be exiles no more, that's not our experience now.

LIVING AS EXILES NOW

So how do we live as exiles now? If we looked for answers within ourselves or on social media, we'd have a different how-to guide than what Peter gives. Here's how he calls us to live during our present exile.

1. EXILES SHOULD BE HOLY.

Exiles should be holy because we've been chosen by the Father, redeemed by the blood of Christ, and filled with the Holy Spirit. The new birth we now have because of the resurrection of Christ affords us the ability not to be conformed to the passions of our former ignorance (1:14). The same power that resurrected Christ from the dead is at work inside Christians to resurrect us from our sin nature. Christians should be holy in all our conduct (v. 15) because our sacrificial Lamb is holy. His spotless sacrifice is what saves our souls and allows us to imitate him. Like Christ, we're sons of God while strangers on earth.

Peter calls us to display our distinct nature in love, faith, and hope (v. 8). Holiness looks like loving God deeply. Even though we haven't seen him, we love him, ultimately because he first loved us and gave us the ability to trust him. What a grace it is to have a faith in Christ that isn't destroyed by trials but is purified and strengthened by them. By setting our hope on things above, on the future return of Christ (v. 13), we're able to live in holiness now as we anticipate the place Christ is preparing for us. The hope of a future home is what enables exiles to be holy.

2. EXILES SHOULD DO GOOD.

Not only are Christians called to be holy, but we're also called to do good works. We're not to become holy hermits who segregate ourselves from the world into a Christian snow globe. Peter tells us to "turn away from evil and do good" (3:11). It's not enough for us to reject evil. We must pursue good works, which God created in advance for us to walk in (Eph. 2:10).

These good works are to be done in the world. As Peter says, "Keep your conduct *among* the Gentiles honorable, so that when they speak against you as evildoers, they may *see* your good deeds and glorify God on the day of visitation" (1 Pet. 2:12, emphasis added). Believers should stand out as Good Samaritans while living among those who think differently, worship differently, and hold different values. God calls us to love our neighbors, and he determines who those neighbors are. By the Spirit we must love and serve our Muslim neighbors, our LGBT+ neighbors, and our neighbors with no religious affiliation. Neighbors who don't speak our language. Neighbors who post signs in their yard that we disagree with. Neighbors who irk us and do things we can't stand.

Our good works shouldn't be driven by partiality or comfort. As Peter says, we should never return "evil for evil or reviling for reviling" but instead bless our enemies (3:9). Of course, this requires faith for exiles who are themselves slandered and mocked. But we can do it by faith as we entrust ourselves to our faithful Creator and Judge (4:19; cf. 2:23). We recognize living a distinctly Christian life is an evangelistic tool God uses to reach those in our path. As they see our good works, it will lead some to glorify God (2:11–12).

3. EXILES SHOULD SPEAK THE TRUTH RESPECTFULLY.

When speaking the truth, we're often focused on what we're saying while ignoring how we say it. If someone points this out, we might accuse them of being the "tone police." But Peter says *what* and *how* we speak both matter to God. When we share with unbelievers about the hope we have, we're to do it respectfully and with a clear conscience (3:15–16). If we must suffer for speaking up, it should be because we've done good and not evil.

Peter says those who falsely accuse us will one day be silenced and put to shame (2:15; 3:16). Sadly, Christians in the public square are often the ones put to shame when they're not speaking the truth or they're not speaking respectfully. If what we say and how we say it is wrong, it may bring suffering, but it's not suffering for Christ's sake.

How many times have we felt like we're suffering for righteousness' sake when, in reality, it was brought on by our own sinful speech? How often has our exile been our own fault? So Peter reminds us to imitate Christ, who has no deceit in his mouth (2:22–23), rather than imitate the Gentiles, who themselves struggle with sins of the tongue when they slander (4:4).

4. EXILES SHOULD LOVE SINCERELY.

There's one passage in all of 1 Peter that references our love for God (1:8); there are four that speak of our love for other believers. Peter says the reason we purified our souls through obedience to God's gospel was for the purpose of loving our brothers and sisters in Christ (1:22). Peter commands us to love the brotherhood (2:17). He commands us not only to love them but to keep fervent in our love for one another because love covers a multitude of sins (4:8). To be fervent in love is to be zealous and earnest because of a shared goodwill, a supernatural affection, and an eternal bond. This bond helps us greet one another with the kiss of love (5:14), which means we accept each other with an impartial love.

This loving acceptance shouldn't be ravaged by political parties, caste systems, cultural differences, or denominational distinctions. Because none of these is our home! America isn't our home. No constituency, culture, or class is our home. No matter where we live, we're not home yet. We're just passing through. We're making our way to an eternal home inhabited by believers from all different backgrounds—even people we disagree with.

Living in a hostile world, exiles can't afford to fight with each other. Instead, we should fight for unifying love, laying aside secondary concerns for what's of first importance (1 Cor. 15:1–4). As we gather around the glorious gospel of Christ, we can join hands with one another, knowing the body of Christ includes a global church that extends far beyond the eyes we peer into each Sunday. It even reaches beyond those who are alive now to a faith that has existed for thousands of years, spans a plethora of cultures, and includes people from a variety of political parties—and even some who choose not to vote. It's a faith that tells us we can't say we love God if we don't love our brothers and sisters (1 John 4:20).

There'll be times we're tempted not to love—maybe because we're offended or there's a disagreement. Rather than cancel each other or question the faith of a brother, may our love be like a thick, grace-filled blanket over the saints to cover their sins, so we can truly greet one another with a genuine kiss of love (1 Pet. 5:14).

TEMPORARY TRIALS, ETERNAL GLORY

It's interesting that Peter tells elect exiles our suffering is for a short time, only "for a little while" (1:6). Wait, what? How can Peter say that? Suffering rarely feels short. Typically, when we suffer, the days, months, and years drag on like a toddler attempting to tell a story. Job said if his grief could be weighed, it would outweigh the sand of the seas (Job 6:1–3). And anyone who's suffered knows the temptation for it to be all-consuming.

So when Peter emphasizes the shortness of our suffering, it can only be understood in one way: in light of eternity. This is Peter's point. His view of suffering had been transformed by Christ's resurrection, and likewise, he wants exiles to rejoice in hope of their future resurrection (1 Pet. 1:3).

As we're elect exiles, suffering isn't the end of our story, because suffering isn't the end of the story for Jesus. His story includes eternal glory (v. 21). And when he returns to make all things new, believers will share in his reward. If we suffer with Christ, we'll also share in his glorious splendor and joy. With an imperishable inheritance (v. 4). With an unfading crown (5:4).

On that day, all the pain of fighting against our flesh, this world, and the Devil will be worth it when we see our Lord's face and hear those coveted words from him: "Well done, good and faithful servant. You have been faithful over a little; I will set you over much. Enter into the joy of your master" (Matt. 25:21). And what a joy it will be when we're finally welcomed home. Never to leave his presence. Never again to experience the agony of suffering. Our identity as exiles replaced with glory. What a celebration there'll be on that day.

CHAPTER 14

EXILE ENDS

Brett McCracken

"Then I saw a new heaven and a new earth, for the first heaven and the first earth had passed away, and the sea was no more. And I saw the holy city, new Jerusalem, coming down out of heaven from God, prepared as a bride adorned for her husband." (Rev. 21:1–2)

IF TO BE EXILED is to be separated, displaced from, or cut off from the place or people we most love, then the end of exile must mean, among other things, *reunion*: the coming back together of what has been, through exile, kept apart.

Scripture's story arc goes from union in Genesis to *re*union in Revelation. We were together with God in the garden then exiled because of our sin (Gen. 3:23–24), cut off from God's presence until Christ purchased our reconciliation on the cross. This turning point set the course for exiled people to return, through the blood of Christ, to the paradise of God's presence. In this glorious reunion it will be declared from the throne, "Behold, the dwelling place of God is with man" (Rev. 21:3).

The end of exile in John's Apocalypse includes vivid imagery of climactic battles (20:7–10), God's triumph over the "that ancient serpent" Satan (v. 2), judgment before a "great white throne" (vv. 11–13), and the fall of Babylon (18:1–24). The climactic victory over Babylon is especially sweet for the exiled church. Symbolizing all the cities of the world (in John's day, especially Rome) who oppose God and are "drunk with the blood of the saints" (17:6), Babylon will be brought to ruin, her oppression of God's people halted forever.

This epic victory over Satan and Babylon sets the stage for the magnificent reunion envisioned in chapters 21–22. I want to reflect here on two interrelated images of "reunion" we see in Revelation's description of the new heavens and new earth: (1) the marriage supper of the Lamb and (2) the "garden-city" description of the new creation.

In the marriage image, God's beloved Bride (the church) finally unites with the Bridegroom in wedded bliss. And in the garden-city image, we catch a glimpse of the city—since Genesis 3 a fragile attempt by a fallen man to create his own paradise—reaching its perfected form in the presence of God, being reunited with the paradise so long ago lost.

LONGINGS OF EVERY EXILE

The author of Revelation, John, is an exile in the most literal sense. He writes from the island of Patmos in the Aegean Sea, where he'd been exiled due to Roman persecution of Christians (likely under the emperor Domitian). No doubt feeling the ache for reunion with his brothers and sisters in Christ across the sea, John writes to encourage his fellow exiles—specifically seven historic churches in Asia Minor. The dual threats of pagan polytheism and Roman persecution caused some of these fledgling churches to falter, but John pushed them to persevere. To the beleaguered, weary, and impatient exiles of his day—and to those in the generations that followed—John's Apocalypse communicates a rousing and hopeful message: God wins in the end. So hold fast.

Though originally written to strengthen and encourage first-century Christians, Revelation speaks to the church throughout its existence between Christ's first coming (already) and second coming (not yet). It's a dispatch to exile-believers in every age.

In every century, the people of God are an *eschatological* people: a people in tension. We feel the tension of a long-distance relationship between an engaged couple— the desperate longing to be with our Beloved. We feel the tension between the earthly city where we're aliens and the city of God where we'll be citizens.

It's the longing felt by the bride who keeps watch at home as her husband is off fighting a distant, dangerous war—her eyes ever on the horizon, waiting for his return.

It's the longing of every exile, wanderer, or refugee displaced from his homeland—his heart haunted by a home he may never see again.

We all feel these exile longings, even if we've never been a military wife or a refugee. These are the spiritual longings of a pilgrim people, and they make the payoff of the Bible's Revelation denouement all the more dramatic.

VERY LONG ENGAGEMENT

History is moving toward a marriage feast. We're living in the longest engagement season ever. This is the picture in Revelation 19:7: "Let us rejoice and exult and give him the glory, for the marriage of the Lamb has come, and his Bride has made herself ready; it was granted her to clothe herself with fine linen, bright and pure." The Bride is us, the people of God. The Bridegroom is Jesus, the Lamb. The wedding feast is our longed-for reunion.

The imagery continues in Revelation 21:2: "And I saw the holy city, new Jerusalem, coming down out of heaven from God, prepared as a bride adorned for her husband." Again, the Bride is the universal church. John uses the imagery of the holy city (a symbol of the community of God's people) synonymously with bridal imagery. And in both 19:7 and 21:2, words of readiness and preparation are central. The time has finally come. It's the moment when the doors are opened, the music is cued, and the ravishing bride—having long waited for this moment—sees and walks toward her groom.

If you've ever planned a wedding, either as a fiancé (man), fiancée (woman), or financier (parents), you know what the waiting is like. My wife and I had a seven-month engagement, which felt long in the moment. But it's nothing compared to the thousands-of-years-long engagement story the Bible tells!

From Genesis to Revelation, Scripture is a roller-coaster marriage story. In the Old Testament, Israel is often depicted as an unfaithful wife (e.g., Hos. 2). And in the New Testament, Jesus refers to himself as a bridegroom on more than one occasion (Matt. 25:1–13; Mark 2:18–20). At the Cana wedding scene, the bridegroom gets the credit for the "good wine" that mysteriously appears, but we know it was Jesus—the ultimate Bridegroom—who miraculously supplied this wine (John 2:9–10).

The gospel story has all sorts of parallels with ceremonial elements of first-century marriages (and contemporary marriages, for that matter). Like a dowry or bride-price paid to secure a marital union, a great price is paid by Christ on the cross to secure his Bride (1 Cor. 6:20). Like a betrothal or engagement, which is followed by an interval of waiting before the marriage is consummated, Christ came to earth in the flesh and made a promise to his Bride that he'd go and prepare a place for her and then come again to retrieve her—after which they'd begin a forever life together (John 14:2–3). In the meantime, we wait for his return—and for that unending Revelation 19 wedding feast to finally and beautifully begin.

Christ is preparing. We, the Bride, are preparing. Both wait expectantly, aching for the reunion that will come in that marriage-feast moment.

Whether you're married and can remember your engagement season, or you've walked with someone closely through it, put yourself in that mental space again: anticipation, expectation, preparation, giddy excitement, slight apprehension, hope. That's the space we're in now.

But then recall the feeling of the wedding itself, particularly the post-ceremony party, feast, and honeymoon: the unbridled joy, the overflowing love, the ecstasy of two becoming one, and that blissful morning-after feeling of an entire future together that's only just beginning.

That's the "not yet" we'll one day have—only infinitely better than we can presently imagine.

ETERNAL CITY

There's something magical about city gardens. Central Park in New York. Hyde Park in London. Luxembourg Gardens in Paris. Any time I visit a new world city, I make it a priority to spend time in its most famous gardens. Some of my favorites are Cape Town's Kirstenbosch Botanical Garden, Barcelona's Park Güell, Vancouver's Stanley Park, and San Diego's Balboa Park.

We love city parks because they bear witness (albeit in a slightly artificial, highly manicured way) to the possibility of organic, interdependent peace between thriving people and thriving land—an ancient beauty that's haunted us since we were exiled from Eden.

When Adam and Eve were banished from the garden (Gen. 3:22–24), they were cut off from its bounty and from the perfect balance within God's presence. An angel barred reentry and access to the Tree of Life, forcing them to build civilization outside the boundaries of God's sacred space. Yet in Revelation, we see the reversal as man is given access again to what had been cut off, "that they may have the right to the tree of life" (Rev. 22:14).

Scripture is bookended by the Tree of Life—this image of God's life-giving presence and ceaseless bounty, where humans coexist with nature and never hunger or thirst. Yet in between the trees—where we now live—cities and gardens are in tension. Disunity and discord reign. Humanity and the natural world coexist in tenuous balance. Ecological degradation and the depletion of natural resources result.

Yet whereas human cities (which create high demand for consumer goods) and nature (which has a limited supply to meet that demand) have been in a fraught, fragile balance since Genesis, in Revelation's vision they're a perfect, harmonious blend, the people's needs fully met by God's abundant supply. Revelation 21–22 doesn't show a city *with a garden in it* but a *garden city*, like one gigantic park full of rivers and trees (22:1–3). Note the rivers of life described in 22:1 flow "from the throne of God." The river doesn't go *by* or *around* the throne but proceeds from it. This is imagery of God-originating abundance. It communicates a return to what was lost in Eden: an ecology of perfect supply that depends entirely on God's infinite generosity.

Just as we live now in the "engagement" tension of a fiancé and fiancée longing to become one, so we live in a period in which the city (human civilization east of Eden) longs to be reunited with the garden (Edenic paradise of God's perfect presence). Humanity's attempts to construct paradise on its own terms have repeatedly fallen short.

The first city builder mentioned in Scripture is Cain (Gen. 4:17), and it's noteworthy his city-building immediately follows his banishment from God's presence (v. 16). Stripped of the *shalom* and security of God's place, Cain is left to wander and build his own city in a hostile world. "For God's Eden [Cain] substitutes his own," observes Jacques Ellul, who describes this substitution as "the act by which Cain takes his destiny on his own shoulders, refusing the hand of God in his life."[1] Indeed, from Cain's first city (which he named Enoch) to the great cities of today—from Babel to Beijing, Nineveh to New York, Sodom to Sin City (Las Vegas)—cities often evoke a certain spirit: if not outright opposition to God, at least proud independence from him. Ellul says city-building is man's "I'll take care of my problems" response to God's curse.[2] It's man's flex against God.

Augustine famously described this tension in terms of "two cities": the City of God and the City of Man. It's a corollary to the "two cities" John juxtaposes in

---

1. Jacques Ellul, *The Meaning of the City* (Eugene, OR: Wipf and Stock, 1970), 5.
2. Ellul, 11.

Revelation (Babylon and the New Jerusalem) as well as the garden versus city tension we exiles have experienced since Genesis 3. In *City of God*, Augustine says the two cities were created by two kinds of love: "The earthly city was created by self-love reaching the point of contempt for God, the Heavenly City by the love of God carried as far as contempt of self. In fact, the earthly city glories in itself, the Heavenly City glories in the Lord."[3]

Indeed, cities today are monuments to man's glory. Aside from the presence of the occasional skyline-dominating cathedral (mostly in Europe) or the jarring *Christ the Redeemer* statue in Rio de Janeiro, God is an afterthought in most contemporary cities. Humanity is the star. From Babel to the Eiffel Tower in Paris to the Burj Khalifa in Dubai, the earthly city glories in the heights of man's technological, artistic, and commercial achievements.

But this glory has a cap. The man-centeredness of the earthly city often promises utopia but delivers much less (poverty, homelessness, crime, unrest, class and racial segregation). Yet the ultimate city—the heavenly city described in Revelation—will be glorious with no caveats. Why? Because the God who makes all things new (Rev. 21:5) will be there, replacing the sun as the source of light (v. 23), his trees and rivers of life ensuring unending abundance.

3.   Augustine, *The City of God*, trans. Henry Bettenson (London: Penguin Books, 1972), 14.28.

Yet nature now groans (Rom. 8:22). Cities weep (Luke 19:40). They aren't what they were meant to be. They've been pitted against each other, yet they're still drawn to one another magnetically. Nature was meant to support cities and cities to steward nature. The garden-city paradise may now feel elusive, but it will come. Our banishment from the closed garden will end, and we'll be welcomed into the glorious garden city of a new world. Civilizational discord and disunity will be distant memories. We'll know a city of perfect harmony and union.

EMBRACE THE WAITING

For anyone who puts his or her trust in Christ, exile will end. Whatever exile you now feel—displacement from home, estrangement from family, ostracism in the culture, dissonance even in your own body—it will one day end. But not yet.

The waiting in exile can feel cruel. But it's also a kindness.

Think about the engagement season. As eager as a bride and groom are to get married, the period of preparation is such a gift. When my wife and I do premarital counseling with engaged couples, we often tell them, "Embrace this season! You're only engaged once. Lean into the theological meaning of expectation, anticipatory longing, and impatience."

There's a special sort of joy that touches our hearts when we lean into longing, when we see the imperfections of this life as teasers of the perfect to come.

It's the joy of being in a beautiful city garden or a national park and for a moment feeling a foretaste of heaven (then leaving with a sense of sorrow: *Will I ever return to this beautiful place again?*). I remember feeling this distinctly when, in 2012, I visited Iguazu Falls on the border of Argentina and Brazil. It was as Eden-like a place as I've ever been, and yet I doubt I'll ever return. That bittersweet, gut-punch thought is nonetheless joy.

It's the joy of spending a day wandering a vast, vibrant, bustling city—each alley and plaza whispering of a heavenly metropolis. But then the day ends, never to be repeated. I had a day like this with my wife, Kira, on New Year's Eve 2016. We were in Rome with six young adults from our church. We walked more than 10 miles that day, wandering the streets of our early Christian forebears. We visited the Mamertine Prison where Peter and Paul were once held, and in the Jewish Quarter we saw the San Paolo alla Regola (built over a house where tradition says Paul lived and taught). We meandered through Testaccio and Trastevere all afternoon and in the evening had an extravagant multicourse dinner in the Piazza Navona. At midnight, we toasted as Rome erupted in fireworks and frivolity. It was magical—a day that felt like a postcard from eternity.

Yet even though this all took place in the "Eternal City," Rome is decidedly *not* eternal, as the ubiquitous crumbling ruins of ancient temples and forums attest. Even the greatest earthly city will come to dust. But the heavenly city will remain. That hope can empower us to persevere today, as it did for Abraham so long ago. Our forefather in faith left his home in Ur to journey forth into unknown lands because "he was looking forward to the city that has foundations, whose designer and builder is God" (Heb. 11:10).

The "city that has foundations" will one day be our home, as it will for Abraham, Isaac, Jacob, John, and all the saints who sojourned and suffered in this life. Exiles now, we'll one day be permanent residents. No need to take photos for scrapbooks or purchase souvenirs, grasping for some token of permanence. We won't ever ask "Will I return one day?" Because we won't ever leave.

And so now, dear exile, take heart: this state of tension is a passing thing. The long engagement will give way to happily-ever-after matrimony. The minor key will resolve to a major chord. Mourning will give way to dancing. Tear-damp faces will give way to glowing smiles. Death, mourning, crying, pain: the former things will pass away (Rev. 21:4).

As Gandalf memorably reminds Pippin in Peter Jackson's *The Return of the King*, this age's present pain will dissipate as the "grey rain-curtain of this world rolls back." And then we see it: "White shores, and beyond, a far green country under a swift sunrise."[4]

The sun will rise for good, and it will never set. We will be home with our beloved Bridegroom, at last, in the true eternal city.

---

4. Peter Jackson, dir., *The Lord of the Rings: The Return of the King* (Burbank, CA: New Line Home Video, 2004), DVD.

SCRIPTURE INDEX

2 PETER

1 JOHN

REVELATION

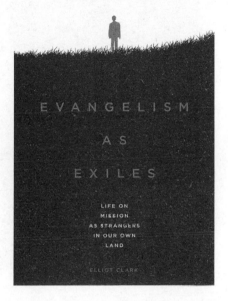

FOREWORD BY D.A. CARSON

EVANGELISM

AS

EXILES

LIFE ON
MISSION
AS STRANGERS
IN OUR OWN
LAND

ELLIOT CLARK

"We are reminded in this challenging book that there is a cost to evangelism, that we are exiles and strangers, that we too often long for comfort and popularity instead of speaking up boldly as disciples of Christ. Clark's book is convicting, reminding us of our great responsibility to proclaim the good news about Jesus even in adverse circumstances."

—THOMAS R. SCHREINER, *professor of New Testament Interpretation and professor of biblical theology at The Southern Baptist Theological Seminary*

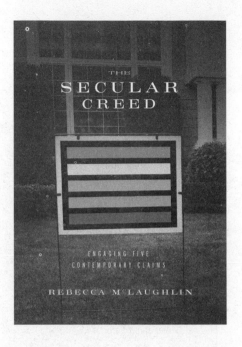

"Rebecca McLaughlin offers a gentle, yet powerful biblical corrective that calls readers to holistic Christian love—a higher calling than the call of the culture, and, often, a harder calling. She examines popular cultural mantras and answers each one with the truth and application of the gospel of Christ. In her balanced and gracious approach, she paints our culture's arguments in the most compassionate light possible—and then shows the beauty of a more excellent way!"

—JASMINE HOLMES, *author of* Mother to Son: Letters to a Black Boy on Identity and Hope

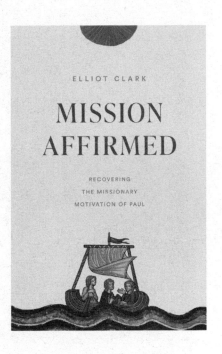

"Mission Affirmed is immensely practical, challenging, accessible, and hopeful. It is a call to be more thoroughly and thoughtfully biblical about why we do the things we do in missions. All of us whether pastors or church members, goers or senders could all benefit from this insightful book."

—GLORIA FURMAN, *author*, Missional Motherhood; *coeditor*, Joyfully Spreading the Word

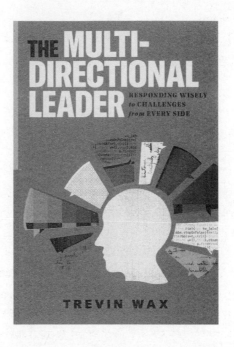

"Trevin Wax writes with keenness of insight, pastoral wisdom, and prophetic forcefulness. In this book he articulates the pressure today's Christian leaders feel from every direction. Wax remains one of my most reliable counselors for leading in a rapidly shifting context."

—J. D. GREEAR, *pastor, The Summit Church, Raleigh-Durham, North Carolina; former president, Southern Baptist Convention*

TGC THE GOSPEL COALITION

THE GOSPEL COALITION (TGC) supports the church in making disciples of all nations, by providing gospel-centered resources that are trusted and timely, winsome and wise.

Guided by a Council of more than 40 pastors in the Reformed tradition, TGC seeks to advance gospel-centered ministry for the next generation by producing content (including articles, podcasts, videos, courses, and books) and convening leaders (including conferences, virtual events, training, and regional chapters).

In all of this we want to help Christians around the world better grasp the gospel of Jesus Christ and apply it to all of life in the 21st century. We want to offer biblical truth in an era of great confusion. We want to offer gospel-centered hope for the searching.

Join us by visiting TGC.org so you can be equipped to love God with all your heart, soul, mind, and strength, and to love your neighbor as yourself.